Drawing a Circle in the Square

Drawing a Circle in the Square

STREET PERFORMING IN NEW YORK'S WASHINGTON SQUARE PARK

by

Sally Harrison-Pepper

Foreword by Richard Schechner

UNIVERSITY PRESS OF MISSISSIPPI
Jackson & London

Copyright © 1990 by the University Press of Mississippi
All rights reserved
Manufactured in the United States of America
Designed by Sally Horne
94 93 92 91 90   5 4 3 2 1

The paper in this book meets the guidelines for permanence and durability of the Committee on Production Guidelines for Book Longevity of the Council of Library Resources.

Photograph and Figure Credits

Museum of the City of New York, p. 50; The *New York Times*, pp. 53, 54; Jointly with Tom Mikotowicz, pp. 128, 129, and 130; Tom Mikotowicz and Joe Mosier, pp. 70, 132–135, and 137–140.

All other photographs and drawings by the author

Library of Congress Cataloging-in-Publication Data

Harrison-Pepper, Sally.
   Drawing a circle in the square : street performing in New York's Washington Square Park / by Sally Harrison-Pepper ; foreword by Richard Schechner.
    p. cm.
   Includes bibliographical references and index.
   ISBN 0-87805-464-2 (cloth). — ISBN 0-87805-470-7 (paper)
   1. Street theater—New York (N.Y.) 2. Street music and musicians—New York (N.Y.) 3. Washington Square Park (New York, N.Y.) 4. Public Spaces—New York (N.Y.) I. Title
PN3209.H37   1990
792'.022—dc20   90-49787
                                                                               CIP

British Cataloguing-in-Publication data available

Contents

Illustrations	vii
Foreword	ix
Preface	xiii
Acknowledgments	xix
1 For Love and Money	3
2 Negotiations and Transformations	21
3 Making Space into Place	45
4 Performers in Place	72
5 The King of Washington Square Park	101
6 Drawing a Circle in the Square	124
References	145
Correspondence and Interviews	153
Index	155

Illustrations

1. Selected Manhattan Street Performance Areas — 40
2. Washington Square Neighborhood, ca. 1850 — 47
3. Redesign of Washington Square Park, ca. 1871 — 49
4. Washington Square Renovation — 53
5. Washington Square Territories, 1964 — 54
6. Major Washington Square Territories, 1980–1984 — 55
7. Street and Other Performance Locations, July 24, 1982 — 60
8. Pedestrian Route (a) — 60
9. Pedestrian Route (b) — 61
10. Pedestrian Route (c) — 61
11. Pedestrian Route (d) — 62
12. Pedestrian Route (e) — 62
13. Pedestrian Route (f) — 63
14. Sociopetal Space — 64
15. Sociofugal Space — 64
16. The Funnel — 65
17. The Spiral — 65
18. The Performance Ring — 67
19. Concentric Rings in the Square — 69
20. The Liminal Space — 70
21. Sideshows and Other Performances, 1981–1984 — 73
22. The Street Performance "Text" — 117
23. Performance Stages of Washington Square — 126
24. Street Performance and Other Activity Locations, September 20, 1981 — 128
25. Frequencies and Durations of Performances, September 20, 1981 — 129
26. Events Over Time = Intensity — 130

Foreword

In this book Sally Harrison-Pepper notes that "much of the history of street performance . . . is found in laws which prohibit it." Like graffiti, prostitution, unsettled weather, and disruptive laughter—street performing is an ambivalent category. As often as not the "authorities" deplore it in their laws while enjoying it on the sly when they can shed their official status. After all, "the streets"—and by streets I mean a variety of public spaces including parks, plazas, train stations and platforms, the front steps of great houses and museums, lawns, beaches—are where people of vastly different sorts are tossed together in a salad of cultures and personal styles.

Even in cultures much more homogenous than late twentieth century America, say the Peoples Republic of China, nearly everyone comes into the streets—the rich and poor, the high and low, the well dressed and the slobs, the old and the young, those out just for a stroll and those looking for a place to transact business—often illicit or illegal. Con artists, lovers, undercover agents, innocent passersby, entertainers, spectators—all have reason to love the streets. Democracy at its microsocial operative level happens in the streets.

The willy-nilly freedom of the streets must be controlled, the authorities say; otherwise public decency will be offended and, worse, the social fabric will unravel. Controlling the streets takes many forms, operates on many levels. The benign cop on the beat barks "break it up" or "move on." But such work is like shovelling sand against an incoming tide.

Street performance in its broadest sense includes organized guerrilla theatre demonstrations such as the building and display of "Miss Liberty" in Tiananmen Square; the impromptu celebrations that marked the dismantling of the Berlin Wall in the fall of 1989; the mixture of gaiety, inebriation, eroticism, and consumerism of Mardis Gras in New Orleans; or the official and quasi-official displays such as the hired clowns selling the idea of shopping inside Macy's or a suburban mall to parades of all kinds—from the showoff of military hardware in Moscow's Red Square to the masked Halloween meander through Greenwich Village.

Wisely, Harrison-Pepper has not attempted a panoptic scan of all street performance activity. She deals in this book with the aesthetic, the entertaining, the mostly non-confrontational upside of street theatre. She focuses her study on one genre—the professional or would-be professional and fiercely independent entertainers working America's metropolitan centers, especially those plying New York's Washington Square. I've seen lots of street entertainment and nothing is better than Washington Square on a hot summer day and evening. The square itself, as Harrison-Pepper explains with elegant detail and logic, is a funnel and a pass-through—designed to draw people in, whirl them around, and send them off again. Located at the very root of Fifth Avenue, Washington Square connects uptown New York with Greenwich Village—in myth if not in fact the art and "free living" heart of a city noted for its arts and multiple life-styles. On its southside the park opens toward Soho, one of New York's newest art and fashion centers. The park is also the campus of New York University—guaranteeing the attendance of young people eager for sun, romance, entertainment, and action. So Harrison-Pepper has picked the perfect laboratory for her scholarly yet lively study of street performance.

The street performers Harrison-Pepper studies—clowns, social commentators, monologists-dramatists, stunt-persons, magicians, jugglers, urban shamans—are key parts of public life under the sun, moon, and street light. Yet they are also often loners. Although street performers are out to make a living, they also declare themselves against, or at least beyond the reach of, the authorities and in favor of the autonomous life lived in the streets. Street performers are consciously not part of official culture, even if many performers aspire to operate within official culture, to "make it bigtime." The key practice of street performers is to "draw a circle" and "pass the hat," to appear and vanish in a flash. Street performers travel light, carry but a few props, no scenery, and very flexible scenarios. Even more than circus clowns or Coney Island side-show freaks, street performers say, "Hey, look at me *for free!* Pay only if you like what you get. And even if you like it, you don't have to pay." They show their skills in a rent-free venue but can survive only if they attract some among the crowds who will pay for being entertained.

By and large the street performers, as Harrison-Pepper shows, function along one of two dramatic lines—making people laugh (comedy) and showing something amazing (testing fate). The comic is typified by Charlie Barnett whose standup routines combine topicality with set gags; the amazing is typified by tight-rope walker Phillippe Petit whose stunts are designed to make peoples' jaws drop. Magicians and jugglers combine the two dramatic lines—one through trickery, the other by means of dexterity. Behind the dramatic lines of comedy and acting against fate—called tragedy when such acting comes to no good end— is a social commentary. The comics are always exposing the seamy, the ridiculous, the erotic, and the contradictory underbelly of authority; and the fate-tempters are saying there is always a way to beat the system, even the Big System in the sky.

The beauty of Harrison-Pepper's study is that she addresses these themes (and more), gives her readers a thumbnail sketch of the history of street performing, and yet anchors her scholarship to an engaging narrative of events occurring in Washington Square. Although Harrison-Pepper surveys street performing in some of America's larger cities—Chicago, San Francisco, Boston-Cambridge, and Alexandria, Virginia (adjoining Washington, D.C.), she focuses her study on New York. In her discussion of Washington Square she relates the history of the park and the ways its different configurations over time have facilitated or discouraged street performing. She combines sophisticated methods of anthropological, proxemic, and sociological observation and analysis with solid fieldwork and interviews. She knows the performers personally and readers get a clear sense of who they are both on and off stage. We learn about individual performers' ambitions, incomes, artistic training, and rehearsals—and get as well detailed descriptions of their acts. We find out how they interact with each other and negotiate who uses what parts of the park when. We meet breakdancers, mimes, jugglers, a turtle racer, puppeteers, an escape artist, a stand-up comedian, musicians, clowns, magicians, and more. One whole chapter details the work of Tony Vera the fire-spitting "King of Washington Square Park."

Harrison-Pepper observes not only the performers but also the crowds moving through the park from morning until well after dark. Using a stunning series of photographs she and Tom Mikotowicz made from the roof of NYU's Bobst Library overlooking the park, she analyzes the flow of people through the park and the specific ways acts gather onlookers and configure them. She charts the peak hours for different kinds of performances. In these and other ways Harrison-Pepper connects the park performances to classical performance theory and practice. She demonstrates clearly that while "the street performer consciously shuns literary theatre," street performances constitute a major independent genre of popular entertainment interacting in a lively way with other forms of performance ranging from night club acts, television talk shows and sit-coms, to highbrow theatre.

In short, Harrison-Pepper has given us what no one before has: an in-depth, readable look at street performing in one of America's premier "found spaces" for such events. This book will be read carefully and enjoyably by performance theorists, theatre practitioners, social scientists—and just plain folks who love to investigate and savor street action. And among the readers, I'll bet you, will be more than a few street performers.

Richard Schechner
New York University

Preface

In New York City's Washington Square Park, Tony Vera draws his performing space on the sidewalk with chalk and writes his name around the perimeter. He describes the circle as "magic," saying, "All I have to do is step into that circle and my crowd starts to develop. It happens by itself. It's magic." Once his performance is under way, up to three hundred people will be crowded around Tony's chalk circle, watching with rapt attention as he manipulates juggling tools, magic tricks, fire torches, and the audience. Nearby, Steve and Carol Mills prepare for a juggling and unicycle show. Across the square, shouts and laughter near the volleyball court mean that another live turtle race has begun, the numbered turtles meandering around a handmade racetrack as Mitchell Cohen supplies an amusing patter of nonsense and wit. Mitch nods to Chang, who is strolling by with a duffle bag full of performance gear slung over his shoulder.

These people are "street performers," a special breed of entertainers who have, for a variety of reasons, chosen the street as stage. They are not unique to Washington Square; in fact, street performers, and especially street musicians, work in the public spaces of many of our cities. Some cities welcome the outdoor entertainer, recognizing the ways in which his[1] shows add a certain exuberance and spontaneity to a stroll

---

1. With the possible exception of San Francisco's outdoor entertainers, the vast majority of contemporary American street performers are male. The few women who perform do so primarily in teams with a male partner or in groups with other women. Too often, women who perform alone are harassed, physically as well as verbally, by men who view them as "fair game" on the streets. The solo outdoor performer will therefore be discussed in the masculine gender throughout this study, not as a generic pronoun but as an accurate portrayal of the field.

through their parks, streets, and plazas. Others, such as Chicago and Alexandria, Virginia, have grudgingly accepted these performers only after lengthy court battles. Yet most American cities prohibit street performance entirely, charging their entertainers with vagrancy, soliciting, willfully blocking the street, or disturbing the peace. The performer is jailed or fined, his props confiscated by local police.

Yet the street performer—joyfully, cautiously, heroically—persists. He juggles, blows fire, performs magic, and tells jokes, appealing both to our sense of humor and to a longing for spontaneity in our city-structured lives. The street performer's popularity is evident in the smiles and laughter of his audiences, the dollar bills in his hat, and the frequency and continuity of his appearances throughout the United States.

A survey of street performance nevertheless reveals a tradition of hostility toward it. Street performance has been described as "a kind of oral graffiti" (Cohen and Greenwood, 1981: 5), the solo outdoor performer dismissed as an "irregularity" or an "unpredictable element [who] seems both to transcend period and to run independently of any phase" (Southern, 1961: 34). In theater histories, anthropology texts, or urban analyses, street performance is viewed as an event that is marginal, inconsequential, unworthy of documentation, even a threat to the image of the city, established structures of commercial theater, or other businesses.

Merchants have long been a primary force against sidewalk entertainment, seeming to feel that its practitioners are unfair competition or that street performance disrupts an orderly civic image. Declared Mike Grosso, executive vice-president of the Fifth Avenue Merchants Association: "The street must be cleared or we'll destroy New York." Urban planner William H. Whyte remarks, however: "It is odd that people who champion the free market are against such a pure expression of it. What is so wrong about solicitation? The passersby are under no duress. They don't even have to stop. If they do stop they don't have to give. If they give, the amount is entirely up to them and their judgment of the worth of the entertainer. It is the latter who has taken the entrepreneurial risk. He should be entitled to some reward" (1988: 36).

But the messages of the street performer are political as well as entrepreneurial. The street performer consciously shuns literary theater, turning instead to the streets as a place of common legislature and participatory democracy. Said street mime Peter Shub: "My purpose on this planet is to instill a homesickness for freedom in the lives of ordinary men. To give people something to shoot for." Remarked turtle racer Cohen: "It is a way of saying, 'I don't have to live my life the way most people do'—there are alternatives." Storyteller Carl Asche, citing Herman Hesse's *Narcissus and Goldmund* as an inspiration for his career choice, declared: "It's theater for the people and by the people."

Street performance is thus part of a larger urban phenomenon Barbara Kirshenblatt-Gimblett called "the folk imprint on the built environment" (1983: 195): the unauthorized, unofficial expressions of the folk, superimposed on the anonymous, mass-produced cityscape. It is nearly impossible, in fact, to separate street performance from the urban environment, for the city exerts a primary influence on both its perception and reception. The shape, texture, and uses of urban space determine behavioral expectations, performance structures, and the theatrical frame. The width of a sidewalk or shade from a tree, the noise surrounding the performance space, the proximity of other performers, the social as well as the atmospheric climates, the civic regulations concerning performance activities—all are part of the street performer's daily, even minute-to-minute negotiations with a fluid and vital urban environment. The setting may even influence an audience's contributions.

Unlike much conventional theater, the street performer works in a "found" environment and must inscribe his meaning upon it. The competence of a successful street performer can be partly measured by his ability to transform city "space" into theater "place." The performer must transform museum visitors resting on steps into an audience seated on bleachers. He must devise ways to invite the total participation of the environment, using its traffic, noise, and garbage as parts of the show. Not only must he allow the disruptions of urban space, he must turn these potential distractions into props, sets, actors for his show.

Street performance is also different from street music. Typically, the musician places an open instrument case, a can, or a box, on the sidewalk and plays music. The collection box informs the overall structure of his show, indicating, for example, that it will take place in a continuous stream of sounds; that spectators may listen for minutes or hours and toss money into the box at will; that participation will be limited to listening, beating out rhythm with hands or feet, contributing money, and applauding. Street music only happens to occur on an urban stage; the larger message is that the environment is mostly to be ignored.

Moreover, many street musicians use signs indicating that they are students working their way through school or are indoor musicians temporarily out of work, thereby seeking to authorize their outdoor performances within a context of indoor work. Sidewalk shows are only "auditions" or "rehearsals" for future indoor concerts.

Street performers, by contrast, are more committed to the streets and more involved with their audiences. There are fewer places for a street juggler, magician, fire breather, or turtle racer to go and thus fewer ways for the street performer to frame his outdoor shows as practice for indoor work. In addition, because the spatial requirements for a juggler's routines or the visual trickery of a street magician's show prevent audiences from entering the performer's space at will, the street performer must develop elements of timing, rhythm, costume, interaction, humor, or plot to attract and hold the restless eye or ear until a "pitch" for contributions can be made at the end. This necessity produces an overall performance structure that is fundamentally different than both indoor theater and street music.

Drawing a Circle in the Square focuses on the street performers of Washington Square Park. It documents the activities of performers who worked in the square between 1980 and 1984. It also emphasizes the relationship between street performers and public urban spaces by including an analysis of the evolution and impact of the square's design. Chapters 1 and 2 examine the street performer's motives, history, territories, and agreements. Chapter 3 introduces the space in which the performances occurred. This survey, of Washington Square Park's history, construction, uses, and rules of action, promotes important links between the physical forms of the square and the kinds of expressive behavior that occur within it.

Chapter 4 presents the broad range of entertainers who worked in Washington Square during my documentation, describing both the transient and the more permanent square performers. Chapter 5 offers a more detailed documentation and analysis of "the King of Washington Square," Tony Vera. In Vera's performances especially, I show how the street performer may become a heroic representative of the hopes, concerns, and fears of those who live and work in the metropolis. The skilled manipulations of a juggler, magician, or acrobat may serve as metaphors for survival in the city, communicating, for example, important messages about a person's ability to manipulate and transform objects in daily life or achieve a sense of control. The street comedian, too, may achieve heroic stature through his ability both to create laughter based on understanding and to present "a momentary and publicly useful resistance to authority and an escape from its pressures" (Sypher, 1956: 241).

Chapter 6 considers other meanings of street performance—to theater, to the city, and to human-space interaction in general. A final strategy employed in this analysis involves a series of time-lapse photographs taken from the roof of New York University's Bobst Library, on the southeast corner of the square. Samples from the aerial photographs, with a discussion of the structural details of the performance event, provide a field-centered or relational view of Washington Square, as well as some concrete information about the ways in which performers must negotiate performance times and locations in the square.

As an interdisciplinary integration of several fields—especially folklore, anthropology, urban studies, and performance studies—the design and structure of this book emphasize a balance between the process of performance in space and the products of the performers in time. It places street performance within a specific community so that we may begin to understand the significance of street performance within the flux and flow of the city. As a theater reduced to its barest essentials, street performance also yields important information about the nature of performance in general—how it works, why it persists, what it needs to survive. As Richard Schechner observed: "To experiment with the space of the whole theater, and to bring the theatrical event into the world outside the theater building, is to investigate most directly the relationships between performers and spectators, and between theatrical events and social life" (1982: 29).

Drawing a Circle in the Square focuses on the complex bundle of performance techniques, environments, motives, and implications of performance as a communicative system within a specific culture. Beyond the interest of the specific material, I hope that the techniques of this study may prompt greater interest in the area of expressive behavior and encourage performers as well as scholars to consider some of the ways in which a social science perspective may enhance our understanding of performance.

Acknowledgments

Numerous friends and colleagues assisted in the conception, formulation, research, and completion of this project. The earliest stages of research were undertaken with Tom Mikotowicz, a fellow doctoral student in New York University's Department of Performance Studies. We took a series of rooftop photographs of Washington Square Park and its performances in April 1981 and conducted interviews and ground-level documentation. Later that year, Joe Mosier and Mikotowicz took a second series of photographs. Portions of this research were first published in *Studies in Visual Communications* (Spring 1984).

Performance Studies faculty Richard Schechner, Brooks McNamara, and Barbara Kirshenblatt-Gimblett offered numerous ideas and suggestions as well as useful criticism. As teachers, colleagues, and friends, I owe each a profound intellectual debt for their vision, support, involvement, and concern.

Numerous speaking engagements, conferences, and dialogues also provided valuable opportunities to extend and refine my thinking. Among these, Edward T. Hall's New York University lectures on space and time, Paul Bouissac's Summer Institute in Structural and Semiotic Studies at the University of Toronto, Owen Lynch's urban anthropology course at New York University, and several American Folklore Society Conferences were particularly useful. In addition, both their published work and informal discussions with Patricia Campbell, author of *Passing the Hat* (1981), and Stephen Baird, street musician and editor of the *Street Performer's Newsletter* (1980–89), led to invaluable insights.

And certainly none of this would have been possible without the remarkable skills, interest, and enthusiasm of the street performers. Tony Vera, the "King of Washington Square Park," endured my near constant presence for over four years, patiently submitting to endless questions and the repeated documentation of his act. Mitchell Cohen and Peter Shub contributed long hours of discussion that affected the final direction of my research. Mitch introduced me to the moral and political dimensions of street performance; Peter gave me a deeper understanding of the performer's mind. Each of the dozens of performers described in the following pages added their shows, their hopes and fears, and their laughter to my project.

Final thanks go to my family members, all of whom contributed their own special skills to the development of this project.

Drawing a Circle in the Square

ONE

For Love and Money

He arrived in Washington Square on Saturday, June 2, 1984, at about 2:00 P.M., a short, dark-haired young man wearing a golfer's hat, high-topped sneakers, and colored suspenders fastened to rolled-up blue jeans. He had a tiny toy camera around his neck and pulled a folding luggage rack with a suitcase and duffle bag. Street performers Tony Vera and Steve Fogelman knew at once that he was a performer looking for a place to give his show.

"What do you think he does?" Fogelman asked.
"Maybe he juggles," Vera replied.
"I'll let you know," I said.

Observing at a distance, I saw him wandering around the center of the square, watching the other performers, pausing at several spots, and finally stopping near Washington Arch. He unpacked his equipment—a dog leash, a camera tripod, a tape measure—and placed a red plastic ball on his nose. He began a series of brief routines: walking an imaginary dog on a leash; measuring distances with the tape measure; strolling beside pedestrians; taking imaginary photographs with the toy camera. He experimented with the opening of the arch, establish-

Peter Shub, Metropolitan Museum of Art

ing it as a proscenium frame for his actions. Few people noticed these subtleties, however. Washington Square audiences are accustomed to flashier performances, and only the red nose clearly identified Shub as a performer.

He tried several popular mime techniques—pulling ropes, climbing a ladder—to attract an audience. Twenty or thirty people stopped to watch. He presented a skit in which he wanted to take a picture of the audience but repeatedly had to ask spectators to move closer together to fit into the tiny camera's frame. He abandoned the skit and blew up a balloon. As he rubbed the balloon on his head, I recalled a childhood game in which the static-charged balloon was stuck to a wall. In Shub's world, however, his head rather than the balloon was pulled toward Washington Arch. A mimed struggle eventually released him from the cement wall's "magnetism."

He removed a beer can from his suitcase and squashed it on his forehead. The audience was impressed until he intentionally revealed it as a collapsing trick can. Shub threw it aside and returned to his camera tripod. As he manipulated its legs and handles, it became a human figure, a woman. He fell in love with it, opened its legs, gasped, looked embarrassed, and abandoned the device. At the show's conclusion, he placed his hat on the sidewalk and bowed. Most of the audience, however, simply walked away—they were accustomed to more elaborate pitches for contributions. He seemed confused and disappointed.

Shub immediately began another show, grabbing the dog leash and looking around. But within seconds, Cotton MacAloon, a Parisian juggler, bounced into the circle, shouting with surprise: "Peter! What are you doing here? How are you? Where've you been?" They talked excitedly for several minutes, then Shub returned to his dog-walking routine. Suddenly fireblower Tony Vera was in the space, shouting that Shub was in his spot and that the police were coming to arrest him. Shub seemed uncertain how to proceed, and MacAloon entered as mediator.

"He has a good act," MacAloon said. "You ought to watch it. Let him do it for you."

Vera finally agreed to let Shub do a show for him, but not in front of the arch. Shub was taken to a location about thirty feet southeast of Vera's territory. He began his audience-gathering routines: dog walking, mime, toy camera, balloon. Vera, MacAloon, and I watched, along with thirty or so spectators. A woman near me said, "A strange show—he's different. I wonder where's he from?" As the performance ended, Vera put a dollar into Shub's hat and left to begin his fireblowing in front of the arch.

I approached Shub for an interview. He was confused by Washington Square and seemed anxious to talk, wanting information on its performers and audiences as well as some reassurance about his act. He told me he had just arrived from Paris, where he had performed outdoors at the Pompidou Center while studying mime with Etienne Decroux. I offered to take him to several street performance areas that might serve his material better than Washington Square Park.

As we left the square, I learned that he was from Philadelphia. He had a degree in social work from Temple University and, while in college, had learned some magic tricks from books and began to perform in the streets. "But I was just doing magic—I wasn't using my body," Shub said. He spent a summer in Paris studying mime with Marcel Marceau and then returned to Paris in 1980 to study with Decroux.

From Decroux he learned to construct pieces dealing with the abstract exploration of everyday objects. His work with the tripod that became a person, for example, emerged from his studies with Decroux. Shub called it his "tripodics"' technique and felt it was his best routine. He spoke of an interest in its unexpected usage: "the way the object points beyond itself; the way the object acquires a communicative function when I use it in a different way than its original meaning."

We traveled to Bleecker Street, Sheridan Square, and Father Demo Square—all popular street performance spots in Greenwich Village. Twice Shub met other outdoor entertainers from Paris. He also stopped to talk to a group of break dancers, who let him use their spot while they rested, and had an argument with a newsstand owner. He gave three performances, earned $50, and decided to quit for the day. We agreed to devote Sunday to finding the "perfect spot" for his show.

We met at the East 85th Street Fair near Second Avenue. As we wandered along the block, he tried the imaginary dog-walking routine several times but never presented a complete show. I soon came to see that Shub used this introductory gambit as a kind of litmus test of the performance environment. If the routine attracted a small crowd, a dozen or so, Shub would then (a) play with the tape measure and (b) attempt to take a group photograph with his tiny camera. If these bits increased his audience, he would proceed with the rest of his show.

On East 85th Street, however, Shub decided his audience was too intent on eating and shopping. We walked over to the Metropolitan Museum of Art on Fifth Avenue, where he discovered an ideal audience: the crowd seated on its steps. (Later, he described them as "Parisian.") The museum visitors were attentive and appreciative of the subtleties of his performance. Following the leash trick, Shub presented the rest of his material in a lively twenty-minute show. Spectators near me remarked upon his skill and humor, noting that he was "different" from the usual Metropolitan Museum mimes. Yet as Shub reached the critical conclusion to his act, he again had trouble with the pitch. He hesitated, seemed embarrassed, and, as a result, received few contributions. When I later questioned him briefly about this part of his show, his answers indicated some anxiety about a lack of control: "In the theater, it's more controlled. . . . I know what's going to happen. I know how much I'm going to earn."

Following lunch, Shub wanted to try performing in Greenwich Village again. We returned to Bleecker Street, where Shub gave an impromptu performance at Bleecker and MacDougal streets. He began slowly, walking his imaginary dog and interacting with a couple seated at an outdoor cafe. Soon, he was in the intersection, directing traffic and mocking a taxi driver. He attracted a crowd of amused New Yorkers on each of the four corners. Then a policeman arrived. Shub was told to "move on."

The crowd booed the officer. "Let the guy continue!" someone yelled. The policeman explained: "Look, folks. He's blocking the intersection. He has to move." But as the crowd again began to yell and hiss, the officer quickly interjected: "But I'll let him pass the hat before he leaves." People applauded (the policeman laughed and took a bow), and at the show's conclusion, there was nearly $70 in Shub's hat. A restaurant owner invited Shub to continue the show indoors, but he declined.

We headed west, to a place near Sheridan Square that Shub had enjoyed the previous evening. In the daylight, however, he quit after the dog-walking trick, saying he "didn't like the vibes." For the remainder of the afternoon, we wandered around Greenwich Village. We ran into the turtle-racing street performer Mitchell Cohen, who offered Shub some information about an audition at South Street Seaport and a possible job at Coney Island in August. They talked about potential street performance spots around the Village, money, and Washington Square. "It's hard to break into the square," Cohen said. "Tony sort of runs the place."

Toward evening, we returned to Sheridan Square. Though Shub still felt the spot "wasn't right," I suggested he try it anyway, "as an experiment" for my benefit. He agreed and presented a performance that attracted nearly seventy people and netted about $40. He was

Peter Shub, Lunch Hour at St. Patrick's Cathedral

pleased with the money and decided to do two more shows before moving on. But he was more intent on duplicating the money than on performing. His performance energy declined, and so did the number of spectators. Shub quit after one show. We agreed to meet the following day, a Monday, to sample the midtown lunch hour crowds.

On Monday, June 4, at around 11:30 A.M., we met at the Public Library on 42nd Street. Though this is usually a prime lunchtime spot for street performers, the city was offering a puppet show on the library steps. We moved around the corner to Bryant Park, but a city-organized concert was in progress. So we traveled across town to St. Patrick's Cathedral. Shub tried his dog leash routine and was optimistic—people stopped to watch, and several sat on the steps. He walked with some pedestrians. Then, standing beside two police officers, he pulled out his tape measure and pretended it was a walkie-talkie. People laughed, but the police looked annoyed. In New York, I had told Shub, the individual officer decides whether a performer stays or goes. Shub made a rapid pitch, placing his hat on the ground and patting his stomach as if he were hungry. Contributions were small, perhaps $15. We tried two more lunchtime locations: the Citicorp Center at 51st and Madison and 59th Street at Fifth Avenue. Both were filled with musicians. Shub decided to quit.

HOPES AND FEARS

Shub's encounters with New York and its citizens illustrate the difficulties as well as the joys of working in the urban environment. Many street performers describe, for example, how much they enjoy being the source of surprise, the unexpected in the urban environment. Said Shub: "In the theater, I expect my audience to sit there and watch. And they expect me to stand there and perform. On the street, they don't expect *anything!*" "Spontaneity and surprise, those are the crown jewels of street performing," observed rope walker Will Soto (in Heise, 1983: 3). "Folks don't walk around New York *expecting* to see me," observed street mime Don Littlejohn, "but they sure seem happy when they do." Urban planner William H. Whyte, describing the street audiences he often sees in New York, observes: "So often they will smile. A string quartet. Here at Forty-fourth! Their smile is like that of a child. For these moments they seem utterly at ease, their shoulders relaxed. People enjoy programmed entertainment, too, but not the same way. It is the unexpected that seems to delight them most" (1988: 35).

Street performers know that it is essential to choose a location appropriate to their style of performance and consonant with civic expectations and demands. Shub learned, for example, that Washington Square Park audiences were unaccustomed to the subtleties of his performance. Yet he found a good audience at the Metropolitan Museum of Art. Shub also learned that police can disrupt performances throughout New York City but that they are more tolerant in some areas and that audiences can be a performer's advocate.

As we traveled to various street performance areas around the city, I saw that Shub rejected spots lacking certain environmental cues, preferring traffic, posters, window displays, dogs, or lampposts to quieter or more orderly environments. He avoided areas that lacked "the kind of audience who'll appreciate my humor." He sought locations with maximum pedestrian density and flow.

Often, Shub spent a half hour or more wandering around indecisively, testing and abandoning a series of locations. He might discard a potential performance space based on an indescribable feeling about it—a feeling that emerged from a combination of his energy level, the weather, time of day, day of the week, garbage on the street, not enough space, people looking bored or stingy. In interviews, however, Shub was confident of his performance intuitions, remarking, "I have a good eye for what works, I always have."

Asked about the way he decided to structure his show as street performance, Shub replied:

> Well, I love the spontaneity of it all, and I hate the spontaneity of it all. It's wonderful and it's scary, because I don't know what to expect and the audience doesn't know what to expect.
>
> I think it's fortunate, though, that the street is still free. In the theater, you have to compromise, and put in what someone else wants you to do. It's got to be commercial. On the street, you can do what *you* want to do and see if it works.

Why do performers choose the street as stage? Ray Jason, a prominent San Francisco street juggler in the 1970s, offers three motives–desperation, ambition, and enjoyment: "Persons in the first category perform on the streets because they can't get hired anywhere else. People in the second bracket entertain on the street corner in the hopes of being 'discovered.' Folks under the third heading choose street shows because they enjoy performing on the sidewalks more than anywhere else" (1978–79: 57)"

A fourth motive fueled many New York City performers: freedom—a desire to be "outside the system," self-employed and self-sufficient. Shub, for example, described the pleasure he gained from being solely in charge of the street event. "The theater may be safer," he added, "but it's also more boring." He clearly relished his ability to control and dominate the actions, emotions, and responses of an audience. He also mentioned the ways in which street performance became a test of his skills as a performer. "The street is still free," Shub said. "You can do what you want to do. The streets are about youth, vitality, aliveness, taking risks." He expressed a desire to give himself to the crowd—to lift their spirits and provide at least a momentary relief from an oppressive civic environment.

In *Passing the Hat*, a 1981 survey of American street performers, Patricia Campbell interviewed Boston's Shakespeare Brothers, who said:

> In what other medium do you have this freedom? . . . There's no other place where we would have the power to say what we please, the way we want to. . . . Basically, all street performers serve the function of creating community and bringing people together, and if we can take them a little bit further and have them recognize our mutual humanity, then it's like going to church, or the theater, or Thanksgiving dinner. (1981: 176)

Many New York performers I interviewed discussed their reasons for performing outdoors by pointing to the freedom inherent in their work. "You can do what you want when you want to do it," explained a New York juggler, "and people who watch really want to watch. Let's face it, we have the most uncaptive audience in the world." Other performers focused on self-sufficiency. They felt that receiving money directly from their audiences both circumvented government intervention and made an important statement about one's ability to be self-sustaining. "No grants from the government," said Carl Asche, "I don't want them. I don't want the government to know I exist. They don't do anything good for me, and I don't want to do anything good for them."

Performers took pride in the fact that the amount of money they received depended upon the success of each performance. "If I do a bad show," Asche explained, "I'm going to know it, because I won't have as much money in my pocket. . . . I get paid on the ratio of how good I am, not necessarily how good my agent is." Performers also focused on the freedom to choose when, where, and how to perform: "Some days I work over here, some days I work over there, some days I don't work at all—I love it!" said a Washington Square mime. "It's not just a living, it's a way of life!" declared Public Library mime Don Littlejohn. The street performer, one New Yorker said admiringly, is "a self-made man."

Many performers also felt that people are more honest on the streets. "If something works, it works immediately and you know it," said tap dancer Jerri Garner Lines, "and if it doesn't work, you know that, too" (in Alexander, 1983: C1). Observed Pat Oleszko, a performance artist who worked outdoors in the late 1970s:

> It is far more cogent to attract people in the public way (e.g. when art walks down the streets and actually competes with the common hustle-bustle) than it is in the arid, austere space of an art emporium. Not only does it force a closer understanding between artist and audience, but it also forces the art to be tougher, more demanding of itself. Street performance affects 90% of the population that may never view art except through the T.V., which God knows is something vaguely akin to using Milk Duds to lighten your coffee. Besides, street performance is the only known cure for cancer! (in Boyle, 1978: 71)

Stephen Baird, a Boston street musician and editor of the *Street Performer's Newsletter,* described street performance as "a kind of positive addiction," telling me: "The streets give the artist a sense of self-reliance, and that's a sense of power that is hard to give up. And it gives you a sense of well-being—you know you can go out anywhere in the world and have a crowd in five minutes. It's hard to give that excitement up . . . the knowledge that I have a certain livelihood that no one can take away from me, and I can do it anywhere."

Many New York street performers described the ways in which their audiences were "trapped in nine-to-five jobs" and pointed to the show's spontaneity as one of its most attractive features. They said their shows presented alternatives to the existing system of governance or conventional ways of living. "My shows are oases of fun and energy in the midst of vagrants, burglars, and traffic," the turtle-racing Cohen declared. Street magician Jeff Sheridan explains in his book *Street Magic*: "The street entertainer is a visitor from a world of no appointments. What he offers the audience is not only a moment of entertainment but also a moment of calm, the chance to pause and share an experience while escaping tensions created by an inhospitable environment" (Claflin and Sheridan, 1977: 127). Architect and urban planner Kevin Lynch similarly remarks: "In a complex society, spontaneity is not often encountered. . . . Periodically, we want to enjoy

Mitchell Cohen

a common, vivid present, enlarged by group expectations and memories" (in Taylor, 1979: 88).

FLOW

Turtle racer Mitchell Cohen once said that when his act was at its best it was "absolutely transporting":

> Every pause, every joke, every nuance is responded to. And it reaches a point where everything I say is funny. The timing is crisp and I can just ride the laughs. . . .
> This chemistry is just somehow produced. . . . It is almost as if I'm not doing it, *they* are doing it. They are getting it out of me. . . . It's beautiful, absolutely beautiful.
> And then at the end, the climax is a *real* climax, a whole purgative and catharsis for everybody—which of course is the crux of why people perform. *That* is the reward.

This is an excellent description of a peculiar state of mind University of Chicago behavioral scientist Mihaly Csikszentmihalyi called "flow." In *Beyond Boredom and Anxiety* (1977), Csikszentmihalyi defined flow as the "holistic sensation present when we act with total involvement"; a state in which "action follows action according to an internal logic which seems to need no conscious intervention on our part. . . . We experience it as a unified flowing from one moment to the next, in which we feel in control of our actions, and in which there is little distinction between self and environment; between stimulus and response; or between past, present, and future" (1977: 36). The experience is fundamentally autotelic, that is, it is intrinsically rewarding and seems to need no goals or rewards outside itself. Essentially, one climbs the mountain because it is there, and the purpose of flow is to keep on flowing.

Flow is an important dimension of many performers' experience, whether on the street or indoors. Actors become immersed in their performance, for example, as attention is centered on the event at hand, and this produces a pleasurable sense of unity in one's actions and awareness. The performer gains a sense of control over the events of the performance. Past, present, and future merge in the unfolding of the show. Yet the ego is curiously absent. As Cohen said, "It is almost as if I'm not doing it, *they* are doing it." A rock climber told Csikszentmihalyi: "You are so involved in what you are doing [that] you aren't thinking of yourself as separate from the immediate activity. . . . You don't see yourself as separate from what you are doing" (1977: 39).

For Cohen and performers like him, street performing is an opportunity to experience flow. They are most motivated by the pure pleasure of their work, passionately explaining that they cherish its immediacy and spontaneity. Remarked Terry Robinson, a New York street mime: "I believe that street performing is definitely one of the most rewarding experiences for a performer. The sense of immediacy in audience response gives the performer a chance to study his work and its efficacy" (Boyle 1978: 43). Robert Shields, while working as a street mime in 1972 in San Francisco, described street performance as the one event in which "there's no barrier, no wall, no hype, no Hollywood. It's probably the most beautiful thing I'm ever going to do with my whole life. It's the purest kind of theater" (in Fincher, 1972: 41). "You just learn to live with insecurity," Washington Square escapologist Jim Gardner explained.

Boston's sidewalk storyteller Brother Blue explained his career as a religious calling. Dressed entirely in blue, he entertained his street audiences with rap-style versions of *Hamlet* ("Ham, a bad brother, disappointed in his mother"), parables, and nursery tales. Claiming an M.F.A. in drama and a Ph.D. from the Union Graduate School, Blue told *Boston Globe* reporter Preston Gralla: "They're hungry in the streets. . . . Everybody is saying: come on, tell us a great story, give us bread, oh, something wonderful so we can make it, so we can fall in love with life. . . . That's why I was born. God put me in the world to tell stories" (1978: 29).

FOR THE MONEY

Yet not all street performers are so lovingly disposed toward their craft. Chicago street performer Milo Max told me, for instance, that he felt "street performing is the absolute lowest form of entertainment. . . . We have to create acts for people with an I.Q. of 40 in order to make our money. I may have—I do, in fact, have strong political beliefs, but I've learned to keep them to myself. . . . Street performers simply provide 'local color' for the gentry."

Perhaps a quarter of the outdoor performers I met felt the streets were at least a temporary "way to pay the rent that beats part-time jobs" (the Steinettes, in *New Yorker*, 1979: 80). Remarked Washington Square acrobat Steve Fogelman: "Sure it's for the money. You think I do this stuff on concrete for my health?" Quipped Moonbeam, a New Orleans clown: "Applause is the performer's butter—but I could sure use the bread" (in Campbell, 1981: 220). Samuel McKechnie, author of *Popular Entertainment through the Ages*, reflects this perspective too, when he declares: "The spirit of open mercenariness is an attractive feature of the performances of wandering entertainers. The showmen do not prate about 'uplift' when going round with the hat. They are offering us a commodity, and if they could make more money at it, many of them would offer to sell us cabbages" (1931: 80).

Yet we have also seen that Shub's more materialist motives would sometimes dampen his performance energy and reception: the more he seemed to focus on the money, the less successful were his performances. Shub's skills were highlighted in novel situations, and repetition simply for cash was rarely a successful performance venture. In fact, a street performer's desire for cash must be appropriately balanced with more philanthropic goals. New York audiences resent being "cheated," as one woman put it, and are far too accustomed to requests for handouts to respond.

But can one make a living from street performing? "I'll just say it's good," Carol Mills answered. "You can squeak by," responded a bluegrass musician. "I make enough," Vera said, quickly changing the subject. "It's good extra income. It's a nice cushion to get you through the winter months," said guitarist Bruce Kaplow. "It could be $2. It could be $50," Chang replied. Few performers would discuss their earnings. Steve Mills said "it's not good to say" what a street entertainer earns.

One reason for the performers' reticence concerning income involves the belief that apparent poverty is at least part of the way street performers encourage people to make donations. "People won't contribute as much money if you're too well dressed," said a comedian, "because they want to feel they're giving money to someone who really '*needs*' it." Popular entertainment historian Brooks McNamara provides historical support for this perspective in an interview with medicine show pitchman Milton Barton: "The smooth talkers put people on guard. 'He's a sharpie, he's a smooth talker.' Once you hear that, you're done" (1976: 25). Street performers, too, must avoid the appearance of being too "smooth." They must communicate messages about money and professionalism which are fundamentally different than those of the indoor performer.

Persistent loitering around representative street performers nevertheless allowed me to estimate that, between 1983 and 1984, the average New York City street performer earned between $20 and $50 a show. Performers in Washington Square, a prime New York street performance location, tended to earn somewhat more than that—perhaps $50 to $100 a show on good days. But let us not play a "multiplication game" with the street performer's earnings:"'Let's see, if he made thirty dollars for this twenty-minute show, he gets sixty dollars an hour, and that's (8 x 60)—Wow! $480 a day! And (5 x $480)—$2,400 a week!' This is nonsense," Campbell declares. "It is not physically or emotionally possible for performers to give of themselves eight hours a day, five days a week" (1981: 221). Numerous factors may affect a performer's potential income: location, day of the week, time of day, weather, performance skills and how well these are matched to the environment, the fluctuating energy of both the performer and his audience, the necessity for breaks, the proximity of other performers, police, and so on. I can say, however, that a good, persistent performer in a prime location usually earned enough money to make other work unnecessary.

WAITING TO BE DISCOVERED

For some performers, however, the street is mainly an audition for indoor work. The audition may last months, or even years, but these performers dream that one day an agent will discover their sidewalk show and whisk them off the streets forever. Street musicians in particular cherish this dream, believing that their outdoor auditions will provide sufficient exposure to land work in nightclubs, concert halls, or Broadway musicals. Most, however, are sadly mistaken. Explained Baird: "Being discovered is a romantic story. . . . There's a whole pile of naive people—anybody who's new to the business—thinking 'Yes, I'm great, I'm unique, and of course I'm worthy, so someone's going to discover me.' It'd be nice if that was the case, but everything takes a little leg work."

Nearly every performer I interviewed could nevertheless cite at least one colleague who had been "discovered" on the streets: Ron Gruenberg, the chain-saw juggler in Venice, California, who appeared on the Johnny Carson show in 1983; Boston comedian and juggler Sean Morey, who also appeared on the Carson show; the comedy team Shields and Yarnell, former street performers in San Francisco; Robin Williams, who performed in front of New York's Metropolitan Museum; NCB "Night Court"'s Harry Anderson, who performed in San Francisco's Cannery Row; the Steinettes, a Greenwich Village singing group, who worked in a variety of commercials as well as the Robert Altman film *Health;* New York City tightrope walker Philippe Petit, a Parisian street performer who later landed jobs with both the Big Apple and Ringling Brothers/Barnum and Bailey circuses; and Washington Square comedian Charlie Barnett, who was discovered by the William Morris Agency in 1983. One street performance group I followed in 1983 had successfully cultivated their skills as business persons and self-promoters to use the street as advertising for their indoor shows.

The Boston comedy troupe Slap Happy created a mailing list from their street crowds and began to solicit work in nightclubs. They then used the mailing list to pack the house with enthusiastic fans. In Washington Square, the street show I saw turned out to be a promotional device. At its conclusion, the performers placed more emphasis on the flyers announcing their evening performance at the Other End nightclub than on their pitch.

Most performers, however, rejected questions about possible "indoor" dreams. "We *care* about the streets," most declared. "I could make enough inside, but I like it more out here," Vera said. "I mean, I'm the King, I'm the Boss out here with my act." These performers have "become the street," a term street performers use to indicate that a performer is either no longer interested in or no longer able to perform anywhere else. It is an exalted position among veteran performers. Only comedians were consistently willing to acknowledge dreams of "being discovered." They discussed the growth-producing possibilities of indoor work—"Indoors you can be more subtle and honest," one explained—and also recognized that the chance to perform in a nightclub was at least a realistic possibility.

ALL THE WORLD'S A STAGE

As William James once remarked, "the passion for an audience is one of humanity's fundamental cravings" (1890: 293), and a number of young performers (as well as some older exhibitionists) were attracted to the trade primarily as a way to gain attention. A man wearing a shoe on his head followed me around Washington Square for hours. He did not care about getting money—he simply wanted me to take his picture. For these performers, the audience is the prime motivation. Indeed, the possibilities for mastering, manipulating, and/or cultivating its responses is a seductive feature of outdoor entertainment. Said Baird: "One of the main reasons I perform is to bring people together and to create contact." Yet as the ropewalking Petit observed, "the artist who chooses this formidable ground of expression faces a tough and savage school. It is the total and constant encounter—*l'affront*" (1979: 58), and the courage to perform outside must be recreated daily.

Cohen compared the preparation for his daily performances to that of a soldier preparing for battle, noting, "It's best to choose your battleground; it's best to choose your terrain." Charlie Barnett used to remark during his Washington Square shows: "Let's hear it for all the New Yorkers who are brave enough to go out and entertain other New Yorkers!"

It is also true, as Petit once observed,

> Anyone can go out on the street and make a show of themselves: three persons will stop to look. Add a whitish face, maybe a clown nose, a few strange props, gaudy clothes: you'll have 20 people around you. Yell, sing, plug in some music, make a lot of noise: there are now 50. Who wait. Who hope. Who grow impatient. And then . . . there is nothing. A street band is lining up its brass at the other end of the park. The empire has collapsed. (1979: 58)

Outside, the performer can test his ability not only to generate a performance but also to maintain it. "Through his performance," sociolinguist Richard Bauman explains, "the performer elicits the participative attention and energy of his audience, and to the extent that they value his performance, they will allow themselves to be caught up in it. When this happens, the performer gains a measure of prestige and control over his audience—prestige because of the demonstrated competence he has displayed, control because the determination of the flow of interaction is in his hands" (1977: 43–44). More than indoor theatre, street performance takes place in the company of others and in the midst of activities that color the event and influence the reaction of those around them. Yet on the street, Shub said, "people are looking—they're *looking*. That's the most important thing," adding: "You know, I wish I could just survive and play on the street. There's so much magic there. There's so much surprise, and surprises make you *look*. The street is still free." Declared a Sixth Avenue juggler: "*This* is where I live! Here! On the street!"

Shub described his street character as "a person who is trying to cope with the world around him, the objects around him," but

> the machines just overwhelm him. Every day, technology comes out with something else, and we're sold on the idea that we have to use it, and we have to use it in that particular way. And here's this guy

coming out with a tripod and using it differently. This machine wants to dictate my behavior, wants to control me, but I control it. I end up opening its legs and exposing it, and then I put it away. I'd like to take a car on the stage and blow it up!

His character seems a close cousin to Jerome Rothenberg's postmodern artist: a "surviving non-specialist in an age of technocracy" (in Benamou and Caramello, 1977: 14). Rebelling against the structures of the indoor auditorium and its conventional behaviors, Shub sought the spontaneity and directness of the urban environment. He was at once fearful and brave. He knew that his unauthorized position on the streets was an important part of his career's attractiveness. "Besides," Shub said, "it's the one thing I can really do very well."

TWO

Negotiations and Transformations

Few cities, past or present, have embraced the street performer as an asset. Instead, street performers are viewed as beings that are "as endemic to cities as fleas are to dogs," says Richard Bruno. "Through most of history, such performers have been looked upon by both civic authorities and the more socially acceptable professional performers as certainly no more desirable than fleas and perhaps not much higher than them on the evolutionary ladder" (in Boyle, 1978: 11). The issue rests upon civic concerns about an appropriate public "image." Yet in fragments, sketches, diary entries, and histories devoted to other subjects, one may find brief references to the kinds of popular entertainment still found in the urban marketplace. Dio Chrysostom, a Greek born in A.D. 40, recalls: "And I remember once seeing, while walking through the Hippodrome, many people on one spot and each one doing something different: one playing the flute, another dancing, another doing a juggler's trick, another reading a poem aloud, another singing and another telling some story or myth" (Cohen and Greenwood, 1981: 12).

A third-century A.D. account by Alciphron of Athens describes a conjurer who manipulated the cups-and-balls trick in the middle of a crowded marketplace: "A man came forward and placed on a three-legged table three small dishes, under which he concealed some little white round pebbles. These he placed one by one under the dishes, and then, I do not know how, he made them appear all together under one." When the performer swallowed the stones and caused them to reappear in the audience, Alciphron wrote admiringly: "He rendered me almost speechless and made me gape with surprise" (in Claflin and Sheridan, 1977: 7).

Much of the history of street performance, however, is found in laws that prohibit it. The 421 B.C. Roman "Laws of the Twelve Tables," for example, outlawed the songs and performances of street singers under penalty of death (Cohen and Greenwood, 1981: 14). E. K. Chambers cites numerous laws and statutes that either forbid performances, equate the itinerant performer's solicitation with prostitution, or declare that the money performers receive is tantamount to robbing the poor. The 1222 and 1259 Councils of Oxford and the Sarum statutes of 1319 prohibited outdoor performances in strong, highly deprecatory language. In 1313, the bishop of Salisbury said that, except for those performers who "sing of the deeds of princes and the lives of saints," the wandering performer is "altogether damnable" (Chambers, 1903: 59). Henry IV's Parliament declared that "no westours and rimers, minstrels or vagabonds, be maintained in Wales . . . who by their divination, lies, and exhortations are partly cause of the insurrection and rebellion now in Wales" (in Jusserand, 1950: 113).

France's rulers feared the *jongleur*, a multitalented performer whose name is translated today as *juggler*. An 1106 law forbade *jongleurs* from certain cities. St. Bernard of Clairvaux declared in an 1150 sermon: "A man fond of jugglers will soon enough possess a wife whose name is Poverty. If it happens that the tricks of jugglers are forced upon your notice, endeavour to avoid them, and think of other things. The tricks of jugglers never please God" (in Claflin and Sheridan, 1977: 48). In 1250, Louis IX banned "tumblers and players of sleight-of-hand . . . through whom many evil habits and tastes have become engendered in the people" (in Clark, 1929: 14).

Efforts to limit or prohibit wandering entertainers persisted throughout the centuries. In 1520, Henry VIII ruled that beggars—a category in which he included "pardoners, fortune-tellers, fencers, minstrels and players"—who were found without licenses "should be punished by being tied naked to the end of a cart and beaten with whips throughout the town or place 'til the body be bloody by reason of such whipping." The 1579 Scots Act called for the punishment of all "idle persons going about using subtell, crafty and unlawful plays, as Juglarie, fast and loose" (in Clark, 1929: 20). By the nineteenth century in England, legislators' views of street performance had reached so intense a pitch that the New Police Act of 1839 even prohibited Punch and Judy shows on the streets.

In the American colonies, a 1612 law in Jamestown, Virginia, outlawed conjurers and actors. A 1699 ruling of the Massachusetts Bay Colony banned all "rogues, vagabonds, idle persons [and] persons using any subtle craft, juggling or unlawful games or plays" as well as fiddlers and pipers (in Collins, 1973: 401). A 1773 Connecticut "Act for Suppressing of Mountebanks" stated, in part, that "no mountebank, or person watsoever under him, shall exhibit or cause to be exhibited on any publick stage or place watsoever within this Colony, any games, tricks, plays, jugling or feats of uncommon decsterity and agility of body, tending to no good and useful purposes, but tending to collect together numbers of spectators and gratify vain or useless curiosity" (in McNamara, 1976: 8).

STREET PERFORMING IN NEW YORK CITY

Yet by the late eighteenth century, "strolling acrobats, conjurors, animal trainers, and other cousins of the mountebank had become a common sight in every part of the colonies." This was particularly true of New York City, where, according to William Smith in 1757, "quacks abound like Locusts in Egypt" (in McNamara, 1976: 6). Declared James McCabe, in 1872: "One cannot walk two blocks in any part of [New York] city without hearing one or more musical instruments in full blast. A few are good and in perfect tone, but the majority emit only the most horrible discords" (1971: 324).

The July 7, 1897, cover of New York's *Leslie's Weekly* displayed a photo-drawing of an Italian hurdy-gurdy player with the following text: "The hand-organ musician is ubiquitous, but he flourishes in great numbers in the metropolis, where he delights or worries the people, according to their individual temperaments. The children in some parts of the town, notably where tenement houses are most numerous, get great amusement to the music ground out by these unwashed sons of sunny Italy. . . . Only churls complain of the interruption of traffic." The magazine supported the activities of street musicians, noting that "at least three-fourths of the people approve of them to such an extent that voluntary contributions make the avocation of strolling minstrel profitable."

The growing sentiment among New York City officials, however, was that the street musician was a beggar, not a performer. Thus, on March 8, 1935, Mayor Fiorello La Guardia turned the city's licensing of musicians over to the Welfare Department, declaring that the city would "no longer go into partnership with this concession in mendicancy" (*New York Times*, 1935: 23). It seems that street musicians were virtually eradicated from the city, for they resurface only in scattered references. The following account of musical activities in Washington Square is the best of these.

THE FOLK SINGERS' "RIOT"

Around 1945, Washington Square Park's fountain area was the regular weekly meeting place for a variety of singers and musicians. Sessions would start around 2:00 P.M. every Sunday afternoon and "go on 'til it got fully dark or people got hungry" (Kornfeld, 1959: 8). The range of musical styles included bluegrass, jazz, ragtime, jug band, blues, and folk songs. Musician and author Barry Kornfeld has firsthand reports of Tom Paley, Pete Seeger, and Harry Belafonte informally performing in the square. Jay Feldman remembers seeing Dave Van Ronk, Theodore Bikel, and Oscar Brand (1983: 21). During my 1980–84 documentation of the square, the fountain continued to serve as a meeting place for musicians.

The musicians received permits to sing or play in the square from the Parks Department. These were easily available and could be renewed monthly. They allowed the holder to play his or her instrument from 2:00 P.M. to 6:00 P.M. on Sundays. Musician Michael James adds that "by tacit understanding" certain parts of the park were reserved for quieter activities or groups (1959: 34). In some ways, then, the square's musical events were self-regulating.

But on March 27, 1961, Parks Commissioner Newbold Morris authorized a ban on the musician's permits. A spokesperson for Morris said the commissioner had "noticed recently that minstrels of unsavory appearance were giving performances in Washington Square Park and then soliciting money from their audiences" (*New York Times*, 1961: 37). Two weeks later, on April 9, 1961, several hundred folk singers and musicians gathered in the square to protest their eviction. They carried placards—"Music Tames the Savage Beast" (Hofmann, 1961: 27)—sang songs, and marched across the space, ending their protest in front of Judson Memorial Church on the southwest corner of the square.

Around 5:00 P.M., fifty-five uniformed officers and six mounted police officers arrived to disperse the crowd, and ten demonstrators were arrested. Several musicians and three policemen were injured. The following day, the *New York Times* reported a "Riot in Washington Square" (1961a: 1). The *Village Voice* responded, in an April 13 editorial, that "there is nothing so painful to the Institutionalized Man as unsubsidized spontaneity" (1961: 4).

On Sunday, April 13, 1961, Judson Memorial Church pastor Reverend Howard Moody sponsored a "Right to Sing Rally" for over five hundred folk singers and their friends. Village attorney Edward Koch (the same Edward Koch who would later become New York's mayor and sanction the frequent arrest of street performers throughout the city) volunteered as one of several attorneys defending the demonstrators. "I think Villagers should now realize this folk singing fight is part of a common cause to save the Village," Koch said. "I think all elements of the Village should pitch in and help" (Goddard, 1961: 13).

More than two thousand singers, musicians, and fans again gathered in the square on Sunday, April 20, to protest the ban. The arrest of a student "nearly set off a riot," according to the *New York Times* reporter Robert Conley (1961: 1). Two weeks later, on May 4, 1961, the New York Supreme Court upheld Commissioner Morris's ban, noting that the folk singers "drew crowds that interfered with those who wanted to use the park for sitting, resting, relaxation and meditation" (Robertson, 1961: 19). Added reporter Nan Robertson: "Justice William C. Hecht Jr. ruled that the Commissioner's denial of a permit was not based 'upon any distaste for folk singing,' nor the singers' clothes, personal appearance, and social or political views" (1961: 1).

On Sunday, May 7, 1961, six hundred folk singers, led by Reverend Moody and Israel Young, again assembled in Washington Square. On this occasion, however, they sang a cappella, having discovered that the Parks Department ordinance required permits only for those singing with instruments. Guitars draped in black were held aloft, and Moody declared in a speech that the ban was a sign "of a city's becoming soulless" (Robertson, 1961a: 41).

Finally, nearly six weeks after Morris's ban was enacted, Mayor Robert Wagner announced that folk singing with instrumental accompaniment would be permitted on Sunday, May 14, 1961, "on a controlled basis," between 3:00 P.M. and 6:00 P.M. "as a compromise between conflicting uses of the people" (Anderson, 1961: 11). On July 6, 1961, the Appellate Division of the state Supreme Court unanimously reversed Justice Hecht's decision to uphold Morris's ban. Commissioner Morris was ordered to receive permit applications from the musicians. Morris said he would grant permits "on an individual basis unless the situation gets out of hand... I never had the slightest hostility toward folk singing or folk singers," Morris said. "I'm a singer myself." Remarked folk singer Israel Young: "We all hope that Commissioner Morris will come down to the park and lead us in some songs" (*New York Times*, 1961c: 11).

CURRENT NEGOTIATIONS

The 1980s are not much different. Laws continue to associate street performance with begging, and arrests are frequent. A San Francisco street performer who rated cities by numbers representing how many minutes someone may perform before the police arrive gave New York City a "12." The street performer therefore learns to negotiate within a number of boundaries. Not only the width of a sidewalk or shade from a tree but also the civic regulations concerning performance activities in public spaces must become part of the performer's negotiations with the urban environment. Performers need to stay up-to-date on the laws, territories, and unspoken agreements between performers and police in order to maintain their livelihood on the streets.

Stephen Baird periodically evaluates street performance locations around the country in his *Street Performer's Newsletter,* providing information similar to the street lore urban performers share among themselves. In an early newsletter, Baird said that San Francisco's shows were "competitive and territorial"; Washington, D.C., performers needed a vendor's permit; summer evenings were the best time to perform in Boulder, Colorado; a twenty-minute time limit had been imposed on street shows in New Orleans's Jackson Square; and the "best places" in Detroit were "sometimes by the train station" and the "Greek section of town" (1983: 2–3). In 1988, Baird reported that Santa Cruz was a "great town," Eugene, Oregon, was "closed," and Anchorage, Alaska; Boulder, Colorado; Key West, Florida; Madison, Wisconsin; and Burlington, Vermont, were among the "good places" to perform. Baird also declared that Toledo, Ohio, and Buffalo, New York, had recently passed laws allowing licensed street performances.

Laws and licenses regulate the *quantity* of street performance in any one area; a city's perception of street performance, on the other hand, affects the *quality* of its shows. In New York, for example, where street performance is illegal, shows are fast and portable—performers must be prepared to make unrehearsed yet profitable exits when police enter their unauthorized stages. In addition, New York audiences are particularly tough, and to survive the scrutiny of the sophisticated New Yorker, the street performer must be especially appealing, captivating, or challenging. In response, New York street performance may be some of the best in the country, but its meaning must be grasped within the larger context of the city.

Richard Schechner, in his essay "Performers and Spectators Transported and Transformed" (1981), describes the way early Greek competitions between playwrights caused the core action of each Greek tragedy—the *agon*—to be a reflection not only of the play competition but also of the City Dionysia as a whole. He further demonstrates that this competitive element has molded the development of plays in the West since that time. Street performance texts similarly reflect the *agon* of the particular city in which they are performed. The street performer offers his performances in the "total space" of the city; it is a quintessential expression of the ideals of environmental theatre, and it works within a space that is charged with meaning. Thus the street performer must be considered not only as a general urban phenomenon but also as an individual who is responding to a *specific* environmental setting in unique ways. Variations in a city's style of street performance

28   NEGOTIATIONS AND TRANSFORMATIONS

are the result of differences in season, city rhythm and style, audience reaction, amounts of available space, the attitudes of police, and so on. The following discussion summarizes the street performance climates of several representative American cities. The chapter concludes with an overview of New York City.

SAN FRANCISCO

Gurus and chanting Hari Krishnas, hippies passing out flowers, encounter groups spontaneously hugging strangers—these are some of our images of San Francisco. The Golden Gate Bridge, Fisherman's Wharf, Chinatown, Haight Ashbury, and Golden Gate Park heighten our impression of a unique, creative, perhaps even bizarre city. San Francisco has a "traditional toleration for eccentricity," says Campbell, and this style has stimulated some of the most unusual street acts in the United States. Campbell introduces San Francisco's outdoor performers by listing "Hokum Jeebs playing the can-can to a cacophony of dozens of chattering mechanical false teeth; Sister Mary San Andreas tap-dancing in a nun's habit; juggler Mike Davis spewing chewed apple and raw egg down his ruffled shirt front, [and] that Baghdad-by-the-Bay landmark, the Human Jukebox," adding that these acts are not only on the "edge of nuttiness" but also represent the spirit and personality of San Francisco (1981: 18). Ray Jason's *Co-Evolution Quarterly* article includes photographs and descriptions of the Butterfly Man, a comedian and juggler who displayed a large tattooed butterfly on his bald scalp; John Timothy, a ragtime pianist who hauled his piano around the city on the back of a pickup truck; Rosie Radiator and the Pushrods, a "guerilla tap dancing" troupe; and Grimes Poznikov, the Human Jukebox. Jason claims that San Francisco's "street corners suddenly blossomed with musicians, puppeteers, mimes, and an entire grassroots galaxy of eccentric entertainers" in the early 1970s (1978–79: 57).

Both Campbell and Jason mention Grimes Poznikov, the Human Jukebox. Poznikov is the best known of San Francisco's street performers. His act has been described in publications as distant as the *Dublin Evening Press* (1975) and as familiar as *Time* magazine (1979). His performance device—a battered cardboard box later improved to a tall canvas and wood structure—was a popular Fisherman's Wharf "landmark" between 1973 and 1983.

The box displayed a prominent sign suggesting that visitors drop a coin into a cut-out opening and push a cardboard flap inscribed with a song title. A popular choice was "I Left My Heart in San Francisco." In response, a trumpet was thrust through an opening at the front of the box and a snatch of the melody played—its length and quality determined by the amount of money inserted. The more money, the better and longer the song. The jukebox also had a coin-changing slot: insert a dollar bill, and a human hand returned four quarters. Poznikov encouraged reluctant spectators with "growls of unintelligible political invective" (Campbell, 1981: 186). Photographers who neglected to make a contribution were rebuked by snarls and shaking as an ancient box camera pointed through the trumpet's opening.

Indeed, Poznikov seemed prepared for each outdoor eventuality, and this emphasis epitomizes a fundamental dimension of all street performance. Poznikov's visitors could interact with the show, experimenting with the box's tune selections or discovering that there was a relationship between the amount of money inserted and the quality of the song. They could watch the experiments of newcomers. Poznikov would provoke and then gratify an audience's interactions with his show and with each other. This is an important part of street performance's appeal: its climate of sociability.

Surprisingly, however, it is illegal to perform on San Francisco's streets and sidewalks. Police have arrested street performers for "willfully and maliciously blocking the street" or "accosting persons for the purpose of soliciting alms." In 1975, the Human Jukebox was arrested for "occupying a public street without a permit" (a permit that does not, in fact, exist). In 1981, Campbell noted that among the five street performance cities she visited between 1980 and 1981, San Francisco's performers were arrested most often (1981: 23). Yet Campbell also claimed that San Francisco was "the very best of the good places" to perform (1981: 18).

This conflicting view of street performance nevertheless illustrates the San Francisco scene: street performing may be a wonderful or terrible experience there, depending on whether the performer is discovered first by an audience or the police. Unauthorized performers are hassled by police and shopkeepers; authorized performers, who have surrendered to an audition structure implemented in the late 1970s, are scheduled to perform in one of the Fisherman's Wharf shopping malls.

San Francisco's system of auditioning performers arose when merchants in the Pier 39, Cannery, and Ghiradelli Square malls decided that street performers were depriving them of potential business. They also felt that the performers were offending their clientele. They therefore decided to "protect the middleclass sensibilities." Explained Paul Levey, a booking agent hired by Cannery merchants: "When I audition, I no longer look for talent; I no longer look for originality—I look for people who are neatly dressed and don't look like they'll be drinking wine or smoking dope in public" (Campbell, 1981: 21).

Feeling that these shopkeepers-turned-theater-critics not only exploited their free shows but also limited or excluded fundamental aspects of their craft, many San Franciscan performers chose to remain outside and develop what one performer called the "modern American street performing consciousness" as a political choice and declaration of independence. A tension between authorized and unauthorized performance therefore arose.

Legislation exists that could protect the unauthorized performers. The 1979 ruling of Judge Rya Zobel in Nantucket, for example, declared that "the requirement of merchants' approval is irreconcilable with freedom of expression" (*Goldstein* v. *Nantucket* 477 F. Supp. 606, 609); the 1981 ruling of Virginia's Judge Albert V. Bryan, Jr., said that "those who exercise First Amendment rights are entitled to an audience that will be receptive to their performances" (*Davenport* v. *City of Alexandria, VA* 683 F.2d 853); and a 1974 Supreme Court ruling stated that "the existence of commercial activity is in itself no justification for narrowing the protection of expression secured by the First Amendment" (*Ginsberg* v. *United States* 383 U.S. 463, 474 1966). But no California court has ruled on the city's possible violation of the performers' First Amendment rights so the distinction between performances persists. San Francisco is a contradictory environment for the street performer.

CHICAGO

Chicago's street performers were victims of Mayor Richard J. Daley's massive crackdown on street activities. Between 1955 and 1976, notes *Chicago Sun Times* reporter Zay Smith, "the only approved street people were commuters, shoppers, and precinct captains" (1982: 62). Bag people, prostitutes, drug dealers, and street performers—people whose activities disrupted the orderly image the mayor wished to promote—were regularly arrested and fined.

Street performers' arrests were temporarily suspended in 1980, when newly elected Mayor Jane M. Byrne, feeling that performance might enhance Chicago's civic image and thereby increase its tourist trade, instituted a "summer troubadour" program. For one summer, the program paid fifty street musicians and a few jugglers, mimes, and magicians $25 a day to perform in the streets. But at the end of the summer, additional funding was not forthcoming. The short-lived summer troubadour program was canceled, and the city returned street performers to their unauthorized position on the street. Declared one frustrated street performer: "Now the city's hassling me for what it used to pay me for!" (Smith, 1982: 62).

The irony of this situation, however, came to the attention of Robert Wynbrandt, an attorney for a large and powerful Chicago law firm. Wynbrandt contacted David Smith, a recently arrested street musician, and offered to help him negotiate a new street performance ordinance. On November 5, 1982, the City Council's Committee on Cultural Development met with Wynbrandt, Smith, several other street performers, and Alan Schnaiberg, a Northwestern University sociologist. Wynbrandt also supplied letters of support from Carl Petrick, executive director of the Illinois Art Council, and Roger Gilmore, dean of the Art Institute of Chicago school. David Smith performed a Bach concerto on his violin. An ordinance lifting Chicago's ban on street performance was passed in September 1983.

Yet this did not end the street performers' struggles. Merchants in the more fashionable shopping districts of northern Chicago (particularly North Michigan Avenue and Rush Street) joined the Chicago Federation of Musicians to complain that the street performers' free shows were "unfair competition." Mirroring the views of San Francisco booking agent Levey, Chicago police lieutenant Robert Wagner declared: "If you have an individual out there who is unkempt, dirty and has an untuned instrument, he's obviously not a performer, he's a panhandler" (*New York Times*, 1983: 2). City Council members were pressured to amend the ordinance.

A revised ordinance was passed in April 1984. It permitted "acting, singing, pantomime, juggling, magic, dancing and playing musical instruments" only by those holding permits issued by the city. It further restricted license applicants to those eighteen years of age or older; limited the hours of performance; prohibited the use of electronic amplification; allowed police to disperse a performer's crowd if the officer felt the crowd was blocking public passage; and declared that a performer or group of performers must work more than one hundred feet away from another performer or performers. Despite these new restrictions, more than 670 performers obtained the $10 license in the spring of 1984.

By summer, Rush Street was one of the most intensely used street performance locations in Chicago. Jugglers, musicians, comedy teams, magicians, and mimes gathered nightly to compete both for sidewalk space and for the nearly twenty-five thousand people who flocked to the area each weekend evening just to see the shows (Richardson, 1984: 8). It was a flourishing urban center, filled with exuberant performers and equally enthusiastic audiences. Yet merchants and police again sought ways either to limit the number of performers or to prohibit them entirely. The American Civil Liberties Union (ACLU) threatened to sue if the city restricted the rights of the performers any further.

But the disputes increased. Jay Miller, executive director of the Chicago branch of the ACLU, said the performers were "great for the city." Alderman Burton F. Natarus countered: "I think the Council was influenced by a lot of theoretical civil libertarianism. . . . I'm convinced [street performing] has a negative effect on tourism and is a blight on the city of Chicago" (Richardson, 1984: 8). Police mentioned crowd-control problems and the presence of pickpockets and prostitutes. By August 1984, an ordinance banning street performance from North Michigan Avenue and Rush Street was passed by the City Council. As promised, Harvey Grossman of the Illinois chapter of the ACLU, with the assistance of attorney Chris Arden, represented William Friedrich and other street performers in a class action suit against the city.

The city contended that congestion on the sidewalk had reached drastic levels and that entertainers added to this congestion and should be banned. Observed urban planner Whyte:

> It was an extraordinary complaint. Of all the avenues in the United States, they could not have picked one with broader sidewalks than upper Michigan Avenue. They range between thirty and thirty-five feet in width. . . . There was, indeed, almost a surfeit of space. The city itself had judged there was so much space it had encouraged the withdrawal of large chunks of sidewalk space for roped-off planting beds. Were these grassy expanses converted back to sidewalk space, the level of service would be higher yet. (1988: 38)

ACLU attorney Grossman further argued that "the fact that these performances attracted such large crowds underlines their artistic validity" (Greenhouse, 1984: A19).

The performers won a preliminary restraining order against the city's newest restriction, but the order contained a "two-year trial" clause. Essentially, the court felt that the city was within its rights to limit street performance when it endangered public safety but wondered if the ban was perhaps broader than necessary. The court therefore asked the city to conduct surveys to justify the geographic and time requirements it sought. Judge Marvin E. Aspen also tackled the issue of breakdancing, a major complaint among the merchants, and questioned whether it would still be an issue when the ordinance was reviewed:

> If it is true that breakdancing has gone the way of the hula hoop and is a fading fad, then perhaps the frequency of large audiences has substantially fallen. . . . Thus, if the City chooses to renew the ordinance next year, it would be well advised to consider the passing of the breakdancing phenomenon in its evaluation. If it has passed, and if—as the evidence showed—most other performers attract only small crowds, the constitutional underpinnings of the ordinance may have vanished for future years (in Whyte, 1988: 39).

As of July 1989, the city had not conducted its surveys and the restrictive ordinance had been allowed to lapse. Chicago's street performers were returned to their customary limbo in the urban environment.

ALEXANDRIA, VIRGINIA

Both Chicago's district attorney and the ACLU's Harvey Grossman used briefs prepared for an earlier street performance dispute in Alexandria, Virginia. Kenneth Labowitz, an attorney for Alexandria street musician Lee Davenport, corresponded with Grossman throughout the Chicago trial, and Alexandria's Assistant District Attorney Barbara Beach sent her briefs to city of Chicago attorneys. Though considerably smaller than Chicago, Alexandria's legal battles therefore directly affected Chicago's 1984 ruling.

Lee Davenport was arrested in July 1981 for playing bagpipes in Alexandria's Old Town district, a small waterfront shopping area. The city had recently passed an ordinance forbidding street performance in its central business district. Shortly after Davenport's arrest, Alexandria officials declared that permits, distributed "at the discretion of the city manager," were required for "approved" performance spaces (Battiata, 1981: B1). Attorney and musician Alan Cohen, anticipating a simple legal negotiation, contacted Davenport and offered to help revise the ordinance. Cohen thought the ordinance clearly violated the performers' constitutional rights of free expression. Yet when he approached the city manager, his efforts at negotiation were flatly rejected. Labowitz joined Cohen in mounting a case against the city. They represented Davenport in a suit for $5,000 in damages.

In August 1981, District Judge Albert V. Bryan, Jr., declared the city's area restrictions unconstitutional (*Davenport v. City of Alexandria, VA*. 683 F.2d 853), noting: "The exponent of the First Amendment expression is entitled to be 'encountered' by those he wishes to receive his or her message. The sidewalk is a traditional place for such expression. Pedestrian flow and turnover is the 'life blood' of the street performer." But as in Chicago, the battle was not so easily won. The city appealed Judge Bryan's ruling and won a reversal by two to one in early 1983 (*Davenport v City of Alexandria, VA*, 710 F.2d 148). Davenport and his attorneys appealed the reversal.

Judge Bryan again presided at Davenport's November 7, 1983, hearing. This time the city offered its defense through testimony by, among others, Alexandria Chief of Police Charles Strobel, City Manager Douglas Harman, Department of Transportation official Chuck Kenyon, Old Town merchant Tony Gee, and urban planner John Pickard. Cohen and Labowitz relied on testimony by William H. Whyte.

The city focused on issues of pedestrian congestion, sidewalk widths, and safety. Whyte, studying the exhibits introduced by Pickard and referring to pedestrian capacity studies by pedestrian planning and design expert John Fruin, noted that the city's figures indicated a comfortable flow rate of 2.8 pedestrians per foot of walkway per minute. (Whyte arrived at this figure by dividing an average sidewalk space of eight and a half feet by the city's figures of approximately 1,416 people per hour, or 16 people per minute.) This figure, Whyte explained, when combined with a notable lack of large buildings periodically emptying for lunch or rush hours, provided plenty of room for both pedestrians and performers. Whyte also described his theory of "self-regulating" crowds, in which people either avoid joining or leave large groups when a space becomes uncomfortably congested. He further contended that the gathering promoted by street performance is not a negative congestion but is instead a form of "small scale sociability." "The presence of street entertainers tends to correlate very strongly with our most attractive pedestrian blocks. . . . The two go together. . . . They give life and spirit to a city," Whyte said (Civil Action 81-709-A, pp. 50–55). Davenport won by an eight-to-one margin, and the city appealed once again.

The final hearing began on August 29, 1984, at the Fourth Circuit Court of Appeals in Baltimore, Maryland. Two months later, on November 1, 1984, the court's three judges, in an unusually perfunctory statement, supported previous decisions in favor of Davenport, awarding him $40,000 in attorney's fees and expenses. The Fourth Circuit judges also advised Alexandria's attorneys not to attempt any more appeals, warning them that the Supreme Court would not look favorably upon a client who stubbornly refused to accept the courts' previous decisions. Alexandria chose not to pursue the case to the Supreme Court, and the decision became binding law in Maryland, Virginia, North Carolina, and South Carolina.

BOSTON AND CAMBRIDGE

Boston, called "the Emerald City for street performers" (Campbell, 1981: 29), is one of the few U.S. cities that welcomes its outdoor entertainers via an established licensing structure. The licensing arose in 1972, when Stephen Baird uncovered an 1878 law outlining procedures for awarding licenses to street musicians who passed an audition at the Police Department. Studying it carefully, he took his dulcimer to the main precinct and, explaining the law to the somewhat bewildered officers there, played the finale from Beethoven's Ninth and an Irish drinking song. He paid $10 and received a license. He soon discovered, however, that the license limited his performances to a few blocks of the inner city and did not permit donations from the audience.

Unable to negotiate the necessary revisions in the license, Baird initiated a letter-writing and publicity campaign. He formed two street musicians' organizations and established the *Street Performer's Newsletter*. One year later, in May 1973, Baird succeeded in having the law changed to read: "Licensee permitted to receive voluntary donations but is not permitted to solicit." The license authorized musicians' performances on any public property so long as the acts did not interfere with the movement of pedestrians or automobiles. Amplifiers were allowed so long as the sound carried less than three hundred feet. (And though the license mentioned only musicians, other outdoor entertainers have since been able to share the musicians' licenses and performance spaces.)

Encouraged by his success in Boston, Baird and his organizations began to petition Cambridge officials for licenses. In 1976, a $2 license was approved. It authorized street performance—defined as "acting, singing, playing musical instruments, juggling, dancing and reading"—in three public areas: the entrance to Cambridge Common, a section of Harvard Square, and the traffic island in Central Square. The license also permitted performances on private property with the written permission of the owner and stated that performers were allowed to receive "contributions of money or property at a performance, provided that no sign requesting contributions shall exceed 12" x 18" in size."

These licensing structures have stimulated a proliferation of street performances throughout the Boston/Cambridge area. In 1980, for instance, Campbell noted that nearly three hundred outdoor entertainers were working in Boston alone. One of the cities' most popular street performance groups at that time was the Shakespeare Brothers, a Cambridge comedy/juggling team who delighted audiences with puppetry, fire juggling, and poetry. Campbell describes a skit involving a dozen volunteers performing as trees, benches, and butterflies: "The springtime skit was astonishing to watch as the brothers freed Bostonians in business suits to wave their arms overhead as trees or crouch as flowers and benches, cavort as butterflies" (1981: 174).

The flourishing prompted by these licenses has its drawbacks, however. Occasionally, Baird has had to intervene in territorial disputes. In 1979, for example, competition for space was so great that Harvard Square regulars had to arrive as early as 8:00 A.M. to stake out a space for an evening show. With Baird's assistance, performers agreed to a schedule of performances. They called their negotiations the SALT (Street Artists Limitations Treaty) talks. Usually, however, the laws of economics rather than politics determine the activities and locations of street performers—it is the public that decides, through contributions (or lack of them), whether a performer should stay or go.

A more important drawback of licensing concerns the effect of civic permission on the style and structure of the shows. The performances I saw in 1984 were polished and slick but lacked the rawness and courage that first attracted me to street performance. Performers could rest easy in their acts, knowing that police would not chase them away. Their performances were longer and had more elaborate stages, with flags and banners, even platforms and painted flats. Shows were praised as much for their sets as for their human performers, reminding me of an old Broadway maxim: "If you can't act, dazzle 'em to death."

Without licenses, on the other hand, the courage to perform must be recreated daily. For many, this is part of the exhilaration of the street. As Philippe Petit once remarked in a 1982 interview: "Finding a spot, waiting for the rain to stop, hiding from a cop is part of what street performance is about, and I hope that this doesn't change." In an earlier *Village Voice* article he delcared: "The flavor of that unique theatre is what attracts me . . . I defend my one-night territory: a corner of sidewalk, a circle of chalk" (1979: 58).

In Harvard Square, I interviewed groups of spectators. "Last week we saw two jugglers, and a magician, and a mandolin player," a couple explained, "but we were late for the Shakespeare Brothers, so we came back to see that tonight." Families had driven thirty miles or more to see the free shows. Performers said they had to focus on "family entertainment" and could not use obscenities or overly sophisticated humor in their shows. Boston and Cambridge performers thus seemed tame in comparison to unlicensed performers elsewhere. Elements of risk, survival, or mastery were curiously absent.

Few New York City performers with whom I spoke were interested in becoming licensed, seeing it as a step toward a regulated life. They preferred a unity that is understood among themselves. After licenses, Petit told me "there would be no place where the street performer could really perform, if what you mean by perform is to express yourself freely." Baird, however, argues that licensing provides greater opportunities for experiment and growth. With licensing, he said, the streets can become a place for sharing and communication among strangers, and this cannot be marketed.

Clearly licensing is a complex issue. On one hand, truly exciting street performance is that which remains outside authorized structures. Its unauthorized position in the civic environment is a key to its attractiveness; audiences recognize and admire its heroic import. Yet the flourishing of street performance in Boston and Cambridge also points to the merits of a civil environment in which the outdoor entertainer is cherished rather than chased. In some ways, New York City offers a middle ground.

NEW YORK CITY (MANHATTAN)

Though street performance is not licensed in New York (its licensing structure was canceled by Mayor Fiorella La Guardia), an attorney in the Police Department's Deputy Commissioner's Office of Legal Matters told me he was not aware of any rulings regarding street performance. Police, he said, just "use common sense" to evict street performers when crowds become too large. In fact, performers have established a kind of truce with the city—an unspoken agreement about where one should and should not perform. Performers should not perform, for example, along Columbus Avenue, where shopkeepers will demand their arrest. They may usually perform, however, in nearby Central Park or in front of the Museum of Natural History. Thus street performing in New York has become an extralegal activity: as long as performers remain in certain acceptable territories—the Public Library, Metropolitan Museum of Art, Central Park, Washington Square—police tend to leave them alone.

New York performers therefore learn to avoid confrontations by congregating in certain areas. In addition, they have learned to develop performances that reflect the behaviors of each area. Manhattan is a borough of economic and cultural territories, each exhibiting a unique style and pace—Greenwich Village, Wall Street, Chinatown, Fifth Avenue, Times Square—and it also exhibits a range of street performance styles and territories. Poets and magicians perform in Central Park; jugglers and mimes choose areas around museums and libraries; musicians work near office buildings along Fifth Avenue during lunch hour; the more eccentric or radical performers gravitate toward Greenwich Village and Soho; below ground, subway musicians and preachers stroll the aisles of a moving performance space (see Figure 1).

In front of the Public Library on 42nd Street and Fifth Avenue, performances are brief—generally not more than five or ten minutes. Shows are designed to entertain office workers on their lunch hour, and performers use the continuous flow of pedestrians to entertain an audience sitting on the library's steps eating sandwiches. One afternoon, I watched Don Littlejohn work a Public Library crowd. He presented mimed imitations of unsuspecting passersby, imitating their gait, posture, or attitude. Many people, discovering they were "on stage" for the audience on the library steps, suddenly became more playful—running, jumping, sticking out their tongues. One man removed his shoes. A police officer, who discovered that his sauntering gait was being mimed for the crowd, laughed and shook Littlejohn's hand. The crowd cheered and applauded.

Times Square performers work the movie lines and theatre crowds. Performances are mostly weekend events constructed for a standing, linear audience. A typical performance involves several tricks performed for a section of the line, passing the hat, and then moving down the line to repeat the routine. Magicians and jugglers do well at these locations.

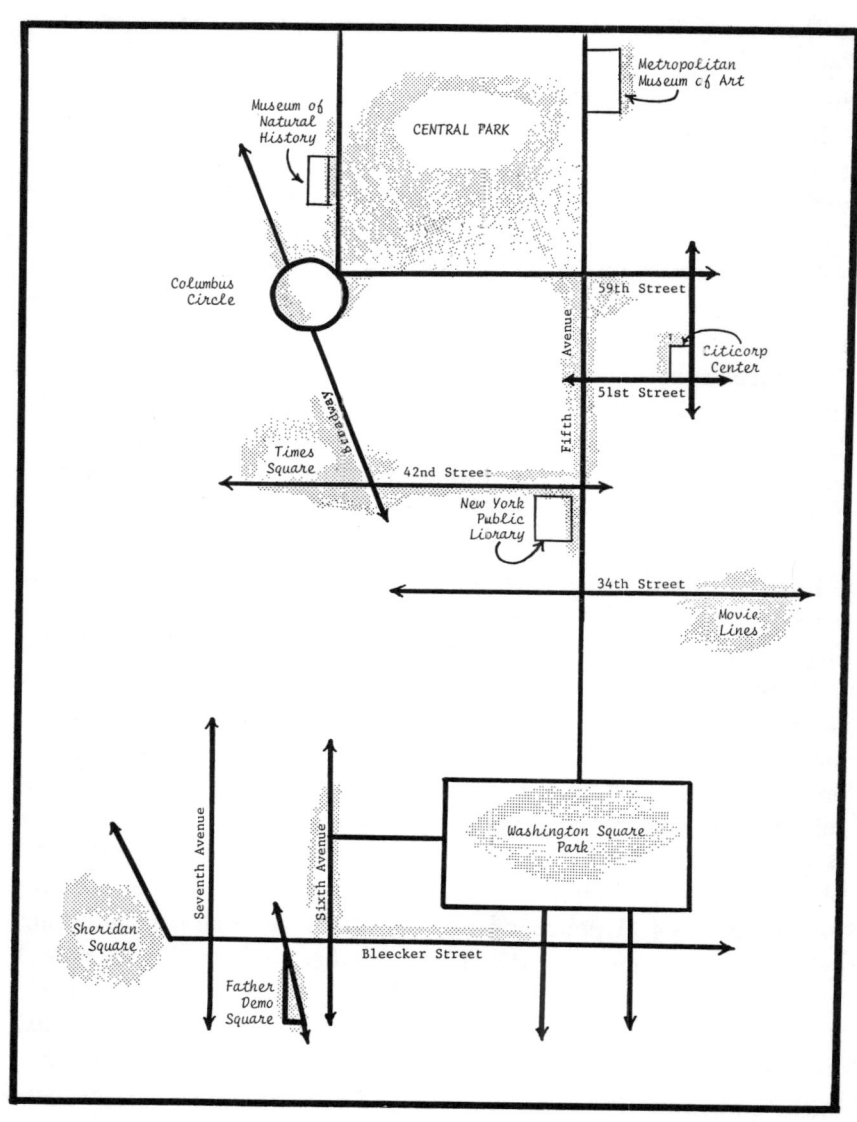

FIGURE 1: Selected Manhattan Street Performance Areas

The Metropolitan Museum of Art on Fifth Avenue and the Museum of Natural History on Central Park West are also good weekend locations, but primarily for mimes. The atmosphere is one of quiet contemplation. Performances are similar to those at the Public Library, using passersby for a seated audience, but may be longer because the crowd is in a leisurely frame of mind. Passing the hat, however, may be more difficult because museum guards frown upon the pitch for contributions.

Music predominates on Fifth Avenue. On a stretch of Fifth Avenue in 1973, for example, one might have encountered "a steel drum player at 60th Street; flutist at 59th; mime at 58th; two girl folksingers at 54th; the Krishnas at 53rd; a trio playing Bach at 49th . . . acrobats, musicians, one-man bands, violinists, karate groups [and] animal acts" (Whyte, 1974: 27). In 1988, Whyte said that 59th Street and Fifth Avenue was "the closest thing to playing the Palace" (1988: 34). The *New York Times*'s William Geist tells of listening to an excellent saxophonist there. A woman put fifty cents in his case. "You're an exceptionally gifted young man," she said. "You'll make the big time someday." "Madam," he called after her, "this *is* the big time" (1984: B3).

I often watched a trio of two clarinetists and an oboe player called "Mozart on Fifth" perform on Fifth Avenue and 51st Street between 1980 and 1983. Their repertoire included classical selections, tunes from Scott Joplin, the Beatles, Broadway shows, an aria from the *Marriage of Figaro*, and country-western songs. They told me they selected tunes that were both familiar and catchy because these drew larger contributions from the crowd.

There are great differences between the outdoor performances of Central Park and Washington Square Park. Central Park is perceived as a serene and pastoral environment for leisure activities; Washington Square Park, despite the confusion in its name, is a noisy, active, urban *square*. Performance activities in each space therefore reflect the atmosphere and tastes of their users. The Central Park performer prepares entertainment for an audience seeking relaxation; "conviviality is the keynote" of performances in Central Park, said Robin Brantley of the *New York Times* (1978: C21). The Washington Square performer, on the other hand, must respond to an environment that is more intense, concentrated, and radical in mood. His act usually includes satire, racial, gay, or drug-oriented humor. The Central Park entertainer may be light-hearted and slower paced. The Washington Square performer must be fast, harsh, and dazzling.

The Parisian ropewalker Philippe Petit was Washington Square's most pioneering and outspoken street performer. His views, published in several *Village Voice* articles and handed down orally among street performers, have influenced performers who continue to work in New York and other cities around the country. Petit taught performers, for example, that "one has to sculpt the space.... The street is not a theatrical place, one has to establish oneself there, to defend oneself there. An imaginary theater has to be built" (1979: 58). He was Washington Square's first "king," and handed his title on to Tony Vera.

Petit achieved street performance notoriety on August 7, 1974, at 7:15 A.M. when, for forty-five minutes, he performed his high wire act—complete with knee bends and walks both backward and forward— between the 1,350-feet-high World Trade Center towers. During the night, he had gained access to one of the towers, shot a rope across to the other tower with a crossbow, and managed to pull a metal cable between the two. Traffic was snarled for over an hour, offices were empty, news crews thronged the streets. "I was dying with happiness," Petit recalled.

Though Petit was arrested for "disorderly conduct and criminal trespass," Manhattan District Attorney Richard H. Kuh and New York City Parks Commissioner Edwin Weisel, Jr., agreed to drop the charges "in exchange for a free aerial performance in a city park 'for the children of the city'" (Lichtenstein, 1974: 20). Three weeks later, Petit walked barefoot along a six-hundred-foot cable stretched across the lake near Central Park's Belvedere Castle as penance for his Trade Center stunt. Petit has since performed with the Big Apple and Ringling Brothers/Barnum and Bailey circuses; walked across the top of Notre Dame in Paris; walked a wire at the Cathedral of St. John the Divine Cathedral; performed for the opening of the New Orleans Superdome; walked between the spires of Laon Cathedral in France for an ABC "Wide World of Sports" special; written a book (*On the High Wire*), which he promoted on NBC's "Today Show" in June 1975; was featured in a film called *Concert in the Sky* for high school students; and received the Sir Isaac Newton Award for Defying Gravity from students of the Polytechnic Institute of New York.

During the Petit era, New York newspapers and journals responded to the street performance craze with a wealth of articles and photographs. The *New Yorker* (1975–83) devoted columns to descriptions of James Graseck, a Fifth Avenue street violinist; Hans, a German cello player on the corner of Eighth and Macdougal streets in the Village; Dorothy Carter, a forty-year-old dulcimer player on West Fourth Street; the juggling and unicycle team of Steve and Carol Mills; Morton Sanders, a Central Park conga player; the Steinettes, a Sheridan Square singing group; steel drum player Victor Brady, who claims to be New York's "original street performer"; and Rubin Levin, a violinist, who entertained Times Square theatre lines.

In April 1977, a *New York Times* reporter described a Saturday afternoon show at the Metropolitan Museum of Art consisting of two mimes, three jugglers, and one combination comedian-clown-juggler. "Most passersby smiled delightedly and allowed themselves to be engaged in waltzes or to be handed mimed flowers. The audience on the steps often broke into applause, and contributed generously to the actors' incomes" (1977: B1). The reporter also interviewed a spokesperson for the Public Information Division of the Police Department, who said the shows were against the law. Collecting money, the spokesperson explained, constitutes a concession and therefore requires a permit (though, as noted earlier, no permit exists for street performance, as a "concession" or otherwise).

In 1977, Manuela Hoelterhoff of the *Wall Street Journal* said that "on the whole, these outdoor entertainers are making this city . . . a friendlier, more cheerful place. New Yorkers who would normally freeze with fear if you began talking to them on the street strike up conversations with strangers about the merit of a particularly intense bongo player or saxophonist." Describing musicians, mimes, jugglers, and magicians, Hoelterhoff concluded that "street entertainers are injecting some welcome spontaneity, humor and color into cities that are too often tense, hectic and impersonal" (1977: 10).

Whyte, too, declared in 1974 that Manhattan has "the best street life in the world" and that street performers in particular are "good to have around" (1974: 27). In 1988, describing the crowd gathered around a street magician, Whyte said: "There is a communal sense to these gatherings, and though it may be fleeting, it is the city at its best." "Good performance and good audiences . . . are the stuff of a good street life," he added. "Its vigor is a test of the vigor of the city itself" (1988: 35, 55).

In April 1982, *Daily News* reporter Bruce Chadwick noted that "so many bands and musicians congregate to play for pay around the steps of the New York Public Library on sunny days that most now arrive by 11 A.M. just to claim a spot" (1982: 3). The *Wall Street Journal* sent reporter Joanne Lipman out on the street with a viola to gather first-hand information. In her October 1983 report, Lipman noted several encounters with the law: a policeman threatened her with a warrant for disturbing the peace in front of the World Trade Center, and she was ejected twice from the mall at Rockefeller Center. Though one might suspect that her musical skills were not as cultivated as her journalistic ones, veteran street musicians confirmed that "the cops throw us out all the time" (1983: 22). Numerous street performers and musicians I interviewed between 1983 and 1985 reported frequent and persistent arrests for "disorderly conduct," "disturbing the peace," "criminal nuisance," and "soliciting."

One week, Mayor Koch declared that the Brewery Puppet Troupe in Central Park was the city's "No. 1 Street Performers" (Alexander, 1983: C24); the following week, a magician was arrested in Times Square and a mime told to "move on" in front of the Metropolitan Museum. I watched a New York City policeman evict a well-behaved folk musician from a subway train. When I asked the officer about his decision, he shrugged and said: "Well, if he'd been any good, I might have let him stay," and sauntered away. In New York, police officers walking their beat are the ultimate theater critics.

THREE

Making Space into Place

Because street performance is so thoroughly situated within the urban environment, a complete documentation of it must include descriptions and analyses of the setting in which performances occur. Washington Square Park's design promotes certain patterns of use, which in turn affect behavior in the square. The unspoken rules governing behavior shape the street performance event in a variety of ways. Pace, rhythm, style, length, as well as the content of each show, reflect the style, pace, and rhythm of this lively urban space. "It is always important to see the shape of a performance," remarks theater historian and theorist Richard Southern. "Our knowledge is hindered when observers report details of an action or ritual, but neglect to help us form a picture of the immediate surroundings" (1961: 58–59).

This chapter is therefore devoted to a discussion of Washington Square Park. I begin with an overview of its history and the origin of certain design elements that remain in the current square. Then I briefly examine the multiple uses of the square and the ways in which these activities have been layered on the space to create a unique sense of place in Manhattan. Finally, I map this place, charting the behaviors produced and defined by the combination of design and use. This analysis is therefore directed toward an understanding of the total environment in which street performance works, for each element—whether concrete or abstract, historical or present day—is a part of the performer's show. The totality of the urban environment affects the reception and perception of street performance in multiple ways.

WASHINGTON *SQUARE* (PARK)

Washington Square is one of the most intensely used public spaces in lower Manhattan, its 8.6 acres constituting nearly half the total public space available to the eighty thousand or more persons who inhabit Greenwich Village. It was estimated in 1980, for example, that nineteen thousand people visited the square on weekends (Wallace, 1980). Within its bounds, people interact and negotiate, watch and participate in a variety of weekend events. Vendors, drug dealers, and palm readers collide with dog walkers, bench sitters, and Frisbee throwers. Bizarre individuals wander about, displaying themselves to any who will watch. A kind of public reflexivity is built into the environment.

It is important to note at once, however, that Washington Square Park is a "*square*" rather than a "park." Notes August Heckscher:

> No form of open space is older than the square. The park is a later creation, a clearing deliberately conceived and then artfully landscaped so as to enhance the city or to relieve its ills. But the square was there in the beginning, more humble in origin than the park, more down to earth in its daily uses. It survives today often at the oldest part of the city, and is inseparably connected with contemporary historic districts. (1977: 139)

Washington Square Park is closely connected to its neighborhood. In fact, Washington Square not only identifies the bounded public space of the square itself but also the neighborhood of which it is a part. Notable landmarks bordering directly on the square include major portions of New York University, Judson Church, the town houses on Washington Square North known as "The Row," and Fifth Avenue.

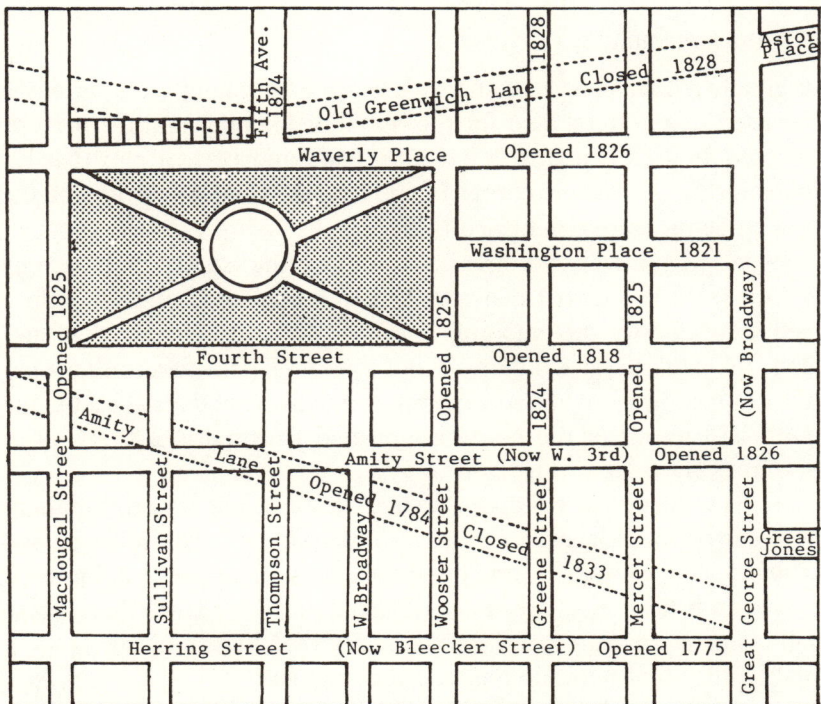

FIGURE 2: Washington Square Neighborhood, ca. 1850

Washington Square's design and use patterns are in accord with several commonly accepted understandings about squares (versus parks):

(1) It exists in an urban context, rather than being detached from it;
(2) It is clearly linked to the street system;
(3) It is based upon a three-dimensional concept, in which it relies on a surrounding wall of buildings to enclose it and give it form;
(4) It is a "mirror of the community."
(Heckscher, 1977: 146–47)

As an urban square, Washington Square Park "dictates the flux of life, not only within its own confines but also through the adjacent streets for which it forms a quasi estuary" (Zucker, 1959: 2). It functions as a "psychological parking place within the civic landscape" (Zucker, 1959: 1).

WASHINGTON SQUARE, 1797–1900

Originally a marshland teeming with wildlife, Washington Square was first used as a potter's field for the burial of the poor and for persons executed at the "Hangman's Tree," a one-hundred-foot elm that remains on the northwest corner of the square. Cholera victims of the 1798 epidemic were also buried there.

By 1825, however, the area surrounding the square had become an important residential district. A new spatial order was therefore needed to identify the emerging social order, and between 1826 and 1828, the square was converted from a potter's field to a military parade ground. In 1831, the square and its neighborhood also became the unofficial campus of the newly established University of the City of New York (now New York University).

In 1852, however, residents wished to construct an environment more suited to their artistic and cultural concerns. The military was removed, and a fountain, one hundred feet in diameter, was installed in the center of the square. Four diagonal paths led from the corners of the square to the central fountain area (see Figure 2). In 1870, a smaller, fifty-foot fountain replaced the original.

In 1871, M. A. Kellogg and I. A. Pillat, the chief landscape designer and an assistant to Frederick Law Olmsted, redesigned and relandscaped the square at a cost of $242,000. Using design principles developed by Olmsted, Kellogg and Pillat added curvilinear plots of grass and walkways, flowers, shade trees, and benches (see Figure 3). Olmsted believed these elements created more pastoral, relaxing environments within the city. Somewhat antithetically, however, the commissioner of public works, William Marcy Tweed, ran a wide street and esplanade through the center of the square, linking Fifth Avenue with what is now West Broadway.

The physical configurations of the new space nevertheless served a cultural and political purpose, asserting the elite's belief in progress through deliberate landscaping, structured activities, and orderly crowds. It represented for them a reassuring contrast to Manhattan's bustling, paved, rectangular streets. On June 1, 1878, the state legislature declared that "the public park . . . known as Washington Square Park, shall . . . be used in perpetuity as one of the public parks . . .

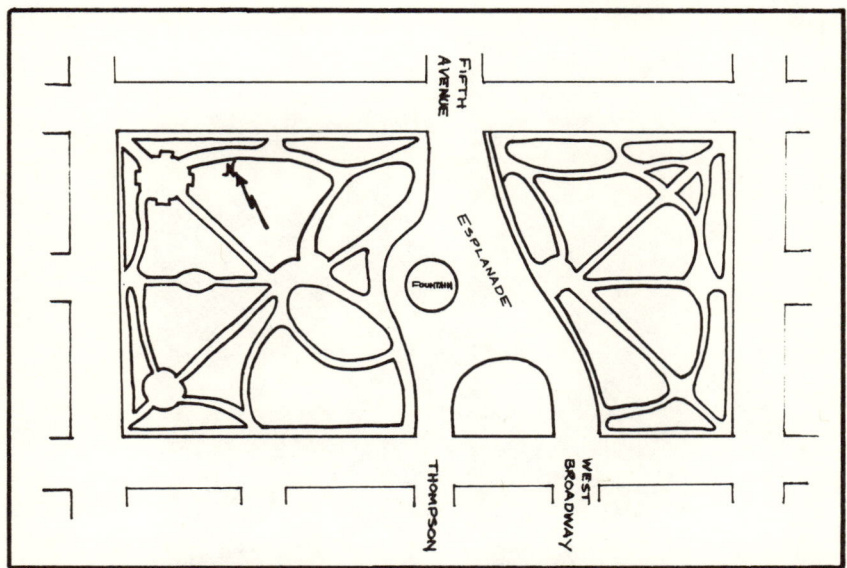

FIGURE 3: Redesign of Washington Square Park, ca. 1871

and for no other use or purpose whatsoever" (in Millstein, 1958: 37). This legislation enabled the square's neighborhood residents to defeat proposals to build both an armory and a federal courthouse on the square.

The Washington Arch grew out of a celebration honoring the centennial of George Washington's inauguration, during which a wooden and papier mâché triumphal arch was erected at the base of Fifth Avenue. Designed by Stanford White and paid for with funds collected from neighborhood residents, the arch was hailed as a "rare and worthy example of public spirit and patriotism" (in Cantor, 1982: 40). The arch was so popular that a permanent white marble version was completed in 1895.

The present arch stands eighty-six feet high and has an opening span of thirty feet. Two marble eagles rest on either side of the keystone, beneath two inscriptions. The north side reads: "To commemorate the One Hundredth Anniversary of the Inauguration of George Washington as First President of the United States." On the south panel, facing the square, are Washington's words: "Let us raise a standard to which the wise and the honest can repair—the event is in the hands of God."

Permanent Arch, Southern View, c. 1900

(I have long felt that this second inscription is particularly appropriate to the square, especially given its present performance activities.)

WASHINGTON SQUARE, 1900–1970

The decades leading up to and including the 1920s were an important period for the neighboring Greenwich Village area, its cafés and literary salons forming an island of artistic activity within lower Manhattan. Washington Square, too, became a central landmark for the avant-garde at this time. In 1916, for instance, a "revolution" was reportedly staged atop the arch. According to Gilbert Millstein,

> Gertrude Drick, a pupil of the artist John Sloan . . . recruited Sloan, Marcel Duchamp, two actors and an actress. The six went up the arch fortified with food, wine, Japanese lanterns, candles, colored balloons, cap pistols, a declaration [proclaiming the independence of Greenwich Village and the Republic of Washington Square], and an iron bean pot, under which they lighted a fire. Miss Drick . . . read the declaration; the food was eaten, the wine drunk, the pistols fired, the balloons and lanterns hung from the entablature, where they

were discovered the next morning, hours after the revolutionaries had descended and dispersed. A year later, Sloan immortalized the coup in an etching: "Arch Conspirators." (1958: 37)

In 1920, Anna Chapin described Washington Square as "one place which is, in a sense, sacred from the profanation of too utilitarian progress" (1920: 31). Another statement attributed to Floyd Dell depicts the square as the "symbolic center of a utopian playground."

In 1930, however, Robert Moses, a man notorious for his "brick-and-tile lavatory style" of park planning, was appointed as parks commissioner (Huxtable, 1943: 2). The climate of the square changed dramatically. Moses, wishing to standardize Washington Square's public spaces and make them more "efficient," added municipal concrete benches, a brick toilet building, stone chess tables, and play equipment packages. These items replaced older and, many felt, more elegant furnishings, and their implementation placed the square in the center of almost constant battles against one or another of Moses's subsequent rehabilitation plans.

One of Moses's plans called for a sunken roadway beneath the center of the square. It was defeated by a strong citizens' group. In 1938, traffic engineer Michael Rapuana planned to turn Washington Square into a rotary, with a formal lily pond in its center. Although $450,000 was budgeted for the project, World War II resulted in the funds being diverted elsewhere. Traffic nevertheless continued to pass through the center of Washington Square on Commissioner Tweed's 1870 roadway, and in 1958, Moses planned to widen the roadway by thirteen feet.

Area committees and citizens rallied to oppose Moses's plan. Residents put up sawhorses and rerouted traffic. The Washington Square Park Committee, led by Shirley Hayes, petitioned the City Planning Commission. Finally, on April 9, 1959, the commission closed the square to traffic (though buses continued to use it as a turnaround at the end of the Fifth Avenue route).

The *Village Voice* reported in 1961, however, that "in violation of the Parks Department's promise," Park Commissioner Newbold Morris was still using the square as a "garage" for buses (Mary Perot Nichols, 1961: 1). Though buses did not pass *through* the square, they continued to use the fountain area as a turnaround and parking area. Then, in 1962, Commissioner Morris planned to "rehabilitate" the square by replacing all remaining nineteenth-century benches and railings with standard equipment. Morris also wished to sow grass around the concrete fountain area; construct a basketball court, skating rink, and bandstand; and expand the children's playgrounds.

The sixty-five thousand residents served by the square protested, fearing that Morris's standardizations would eradicate the last physical symbols of the square's unique sense of place. Several articles appeared in the *Village Voice*, including two by architect and urban planner Robert Nichols, who strongly opposed Morris's plans. Nichols wrote of the dangers of "municipal hybridization," an "invisible erosion," whose "bastardization and debasement of parks will lead to the obsolescence of the whole scheme" of Washington Square (1962: 1). "The fact is that parks and squares are ephemeral objects. They are like litmus paper, registering the exuberance or decay of the communities that surround them. But what," Nichols asked, "has the community been struggling to preserve in Washington Square Park? What kind of park does it have in mind?" (1962a: 6).

To make the Village's intentions clear, a set of "principles" were developed, under the leadership of Anthony Dapolita, chairman of the Greenwich Village Planning Board. As submitted to Commissioner Morris, these principles essentially stated that the square should "retain its unusual character as a focal point of the Village" (Stengren, 1963: 35). Yet more than a year later, residents and Parks Department officials were still arguing over the plans for the square. Should the square be entirely redesigned, partially redesigned, or simply "spruced up"?

In September 1964, Gilmore Clarke, an architect hired by Commissioner Morris, proposed that the fountain be moved into a direct line with the arch, a neo-Greek colonnade be erected at the south entrance to the square, and the lawns be more consciously landscaped. The plan was drawn from the French classic style known as Beaux Arts and focused on symmetry and look-alike parts. It was immediately attacked by the Washington Square community as "too formal" (Sibley, 1964: 33).

Finally, on October 27, 1964, Mayor Wagner accepted a collaborative plan from nine architects who proposed to "rehabilitate Washington Square Park while retaining its basic character" (Benjamin, 1964: 47). Nichols was one of the architects. They closed the square to

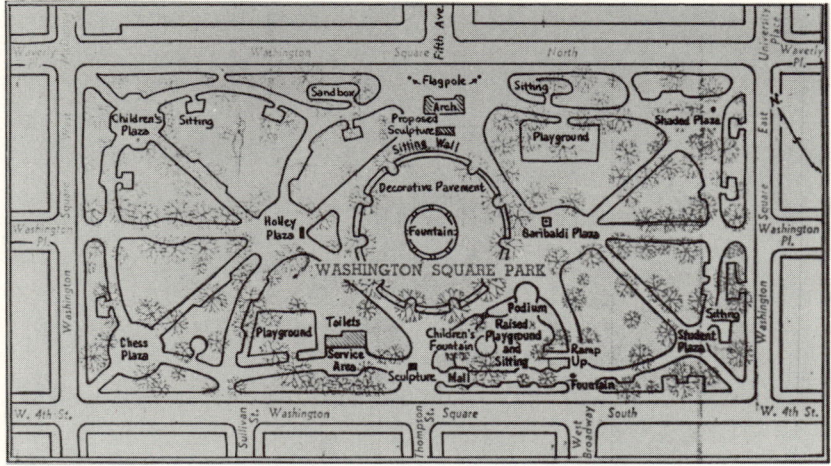

FIGURE 4: Washington Square Renovation

Fifth Avenue buses; added scattered sculpture, trees, and shrubs; installed a new playground and a podium for concerts; and created several sitting areas off the main paths which would draw persons from the heavily used fountain area. Ada Louise Huxtable said the plan was a "test case in park planning," noting that it served "specific local needs, tastes, and traditions" rather than functioning as a "standard design for any park" (1964: 48). The renovation was completed on December 6, 1970, at a cost of $1,559,900 and remains in place in the current square (see Figure 4).

FROM SPACE TO PLACE

The renovations of the square affect and direct behaviors within it, shaping attitudes and group identity. Like a palimpsest, an ancient parchment repeatedly erased and written upon over the centuries, the physical environment and its concrete structures have been erased and reinscribed over time, each change designed to suit the shifting tastes of its users. The square has thus become a kind of "laminated space," with multiple meanings and activities layered upon it.

Yet certain patterns emerge. Millstein, for example, in a 1958 *New York Times* article on Washington Square, described it as a "tranquil oasis with a stormy past": "On week days, it is dominated by mothers and their children; by university students, who use it as a campus;

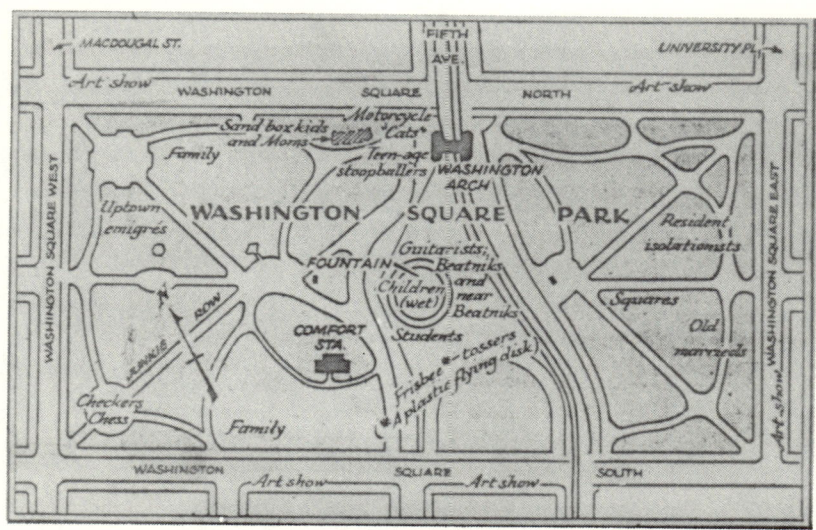

FIGURE 5: Washington Square Territories, 1964

by those who work at night or on their own; by dogwalkers, the old, the unemployed and the defeated. . . . The loudest noises are the squeak of baby carriages and the exhausts of the Fifth Avenue buses" (1958: 32). These weekday uses persist in the present day.

Millstein also notes that the scene on Sundays was altogether different: "On that day, the rigid difference of purpose that exists between the east side and the west side of the square becomes evident. East is for quiet. West is the center of the social life of the square. That life radiates out from the fountain, fifty feet in diameter." The reader may recall the earlier discussion of the "Folk Singers' Riot" and the behaviors on the square. Millstein, describing the Sunday folk singers, punch ball players, residents, and tourists who collected around the fountain's rim, adds that "before sitting on the rim, it is customary to take one circuit of the fountain, counter-clockwise" (1958: 35). This behavior, too, endures in the present day.

In June 1964, Gay Talese marveled at how different groups succeeded in getting along together in the square (see Figure 5). The east side, Talese noted, "is for old marrieds and resident isolationists" (1964: 31). Motorcyclists gathered on the northern curb to inspect each other's vehicles. Stoopball players dominated the arch, while children and folk singers shared the fountain area. West of the fountain, Talese said, was a path known as "Junkie Row." Tourists tended to gather on

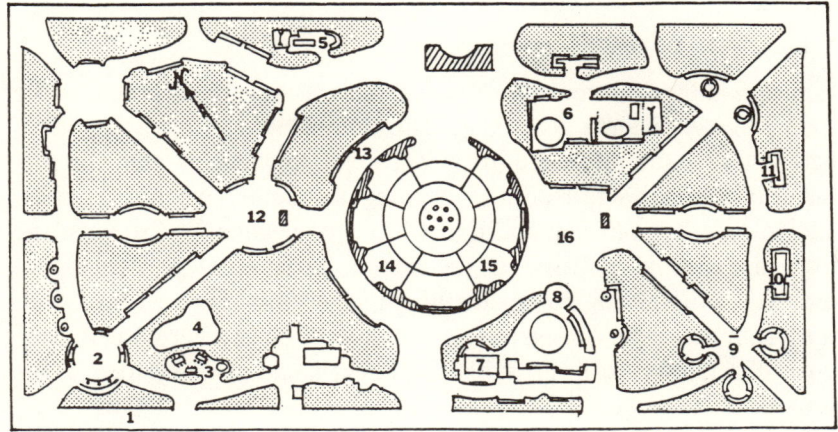

1. Jogging
2. Chess tables
3. Card tables
4. Skateboarding hill
5. Playground equipment
6. Playground equipment
7. Petanque court
8. Podium
9. Conversation pits
10. Italian mandolin players
11. Bluegrass musicians
12. Holly Plaza—"the Pharmacy"
13. The elderly's bench
14. Soccer
15. Frisbee
16. Roller skating

FIGURE 6: Major Washington Square Territories, 1980–1984

benches behind the Garibaldi statue. Talese called the square "eight acres of sociology" (1964: 31).

Notions of territoriality and the divisions between quiet and noisy activities, old and young, tourists and residents, remain clear in the present square (see Figure 6). Washington Square has become "an extraordinary example of cooperation on a large scale with a minimum of formal control" (Kirshenblatt-Gimblett, 1983: 199). Its communicative displays occur within a complex mosaic of highly ordered, clearly territorialized areas. One area is used by children, another by men, a third by the elderly. Some areas are used by French speakers, others by Greeks or Brazilians. Each region features behaviors cued by local custom and successive transformations. Each territory provides a frame in which group identity may be expressed and maintained. Each area has also been established primarily through use and occupancy, through unspoken agreements and tacit understandings among square users. The meaning of the built environment therefore exists in an emergent relationship located temporally as well as spatially.

TERRITORIES IN PLACE

Figure 6 shows the major territories and activities I observed in the square between 1980 and 1984. The dominant territories are numbered. Other, unnumbered areas were used more generally, for picnicking, sunbathing, reading, listening to radios, meeting friends, and so on, thus offering additional levels of negotiation between the fixed and flexible territories of the square. Areas merged, overlapped, moved, or dissolved, but each shift in space was more a function of time than the result of aggression. Fieldwork, however, revealed three types of territory I call the public, secondary, and primary areas of the square.

Public territories were mostly established as a result of permanent design elements: chess tables; an asphalt hill for skateboarding; playground equipment; a petanque court; a podium apparently intended for concerts that was used only once in the course of my observations; three circular conversation pits near New York University; and several rectangular enclaves on the eastern boundary, one of which was used by a group of Italian mandolin players and another by bluegrass musicians. Activities, rather than groups, identified these areas' uses.

Secondary territories were used by a specific group rather than for a specific activity and were therefore under greater individual control than the public territories. West of the fountain, for example, Holly Plaza, known as the "Pharmacy," was the center of the square's drug-dealing activity. It was dominated by three or four drug dealers who regularly patrolled the concrete plaza. The territorialized identity of the space meant that the dealers rarely had to solicit business actively because most people knew where to go and what to buy when they got there.

Another secondary territory was located in a southwest section of the fountain area where a group of Jamaicans held regular soccer matches, using wire trash baskets as goal posts. The focused energy of their game often threatened the physical welfare of any passersby who wandered through the space unaware of its unofficial designation as a soccer field. Frisbee players dominated the southeast section of the fountain's ring. Visiting street performers occasionally tried to work in

Petanque Players

each of these areas, but repeated assaults with soccer balls or Frisbees soon convinced them to move elsewhere.

The square's eldery visitors colonized a bench on the northwest side of the fountain. "It's sunnier here," one explained. "I know I'll find my friends here," said another. "I *always* sit here," responded a third, looking both surprised and slightly annoyed by my questions. Newcomers, unaware of the elderly's tacit boundaries, sometimes invaded the space by sitting on the bench. I watched the nonverbal responses of its more "authorized" occupants: the bench's senior citizens either leaned toward the newcomer and placed shopping bags and parcels uncomfortably close to the intruder's personal space, thus making the unwanted visitor draw his or her limbs and belongings in, or the seniors would move away from the invader to create an uncomfortable feeling of isolation. Sometimes, members of the "bench club" talked across the interloper as if he or she were invisible. Soon, the invader left the space, often choosing to sit elsewhere in the square.

Irwin Altman and Martin Chemers discuss the tendency to expropriate public spaces as an aspect of collective behavior: "People put

The "Elderly's Bench"

their personal stamp on places not only to regulate access to others but simultaneously to present themselves to others, to express what they are and what they believe, and thereby, to establish their distinctiveness and uniqueness" (1980: 143). Secondary territories in Washington Square thus served as a way to create and maintain group identity in a diverse urban environment.

Primary territories were the most controlled areas of the three. Found inside the area I call the "Performance Ring"—the large circular area surrounding the fountain—the primary territories were used almost exclusively by street performers. The fireblowing Vera held the square's prime location, directly south of Washington Arch. Charlie Barnett used the basin of the dry fountain as a concrete amphitheater. In 1982, Chang moved from Holly Plaza into the Performance Ring and established a permanent territory there. Steve and Carol Mills alternated between one section of flat sidewalk north of the Performance Ring and another to the east. Mitchell Cohen worked in an area east of the volleyball/roller skating court, near the Garibaldi statue. More flexible positions around the edges of the Performance Ring were used by visiting or infrequent performers.

Each area was controlled on a permanent and regular basis through a single performer's consistent use of the space as well as through a system of agreements that were supervised by the "King of Washington Square Park," Tony Vera, who said: "I'm the King, I'm the Boss out here with my act. I mean, I have a lot of power—I inherited this job from Philippe Petit. He gave it to me when he left to do the circus." Performers said they reached their agreements through a system of necessary cooperation in which Vera functioned as supervisor out of "respect." "Tony's been here the longest," Steve Mills said. "And he's a really good performer," Carol Mills added. Vera described the territoriality of the square as a matter of "turf," adding that his job was to maintain a level of "professionalism." "I'm the boss," Vera said, "but we're all having a good time. There's no violence." Asked about a permit, Vera responded: "I have a permit, but not legally. Get it? I have a permit by the Parks Department because they like me. They want me here. NYU wants me here. 'Cause I make people happy in the circle. My act's not offensive, they have a good time, and then they give me money 'cause they're having a good time." The street performers' presence in this area affected behaviors throughout the square.

MAPPING "PLACE"

In July and August 1982, I followed more than two hundred people entering the square to determine both major areas of activity and the orbits or habitual pathways of the square's visitors. I selected entrants based on variations in age, sex, race, nationality, demeanor, or social grouping and traced their paths on a map of the square, pausing when they paused, sitting nearby if they chose to remain on a bench, and using a stopwatch to time the length of each stay. They would pause either to reassess the environment, change direction, look for friends, or, most often, watch a street performer. The stationary positions of the performers affected and directed the orbits of more than half the visitors I followed. In addition, nearly three-quarters of my subjects exited in areas adjacent to their entrance, as if they had gone out of their way to walk through the square on the way to someplace else.

Figure 7 shows the locations of street performers on July 24, 1982. Figures 8 through 13 show the routes of some representative subjects. Pauses, indicated by an "x," are explained beneath each map.

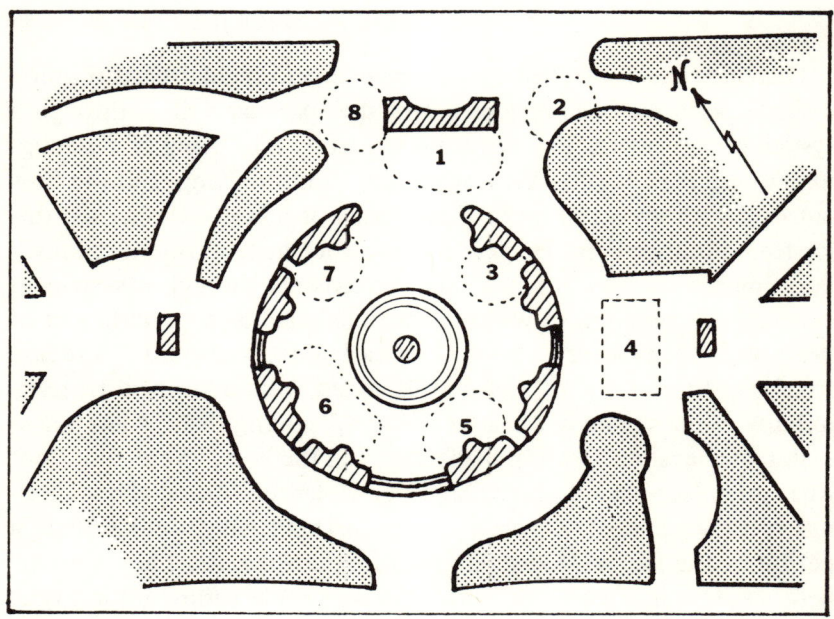

1. Tony Vera
2. Reggae music
3. Rock musicians
4. Steve and Carol Mills
5. Juggler (with fire)
6. Soccer players
7. Jazz musicians
8. Comedian/magician

FIGURE 7: Street and Other Performance Locations, July 24, 1982

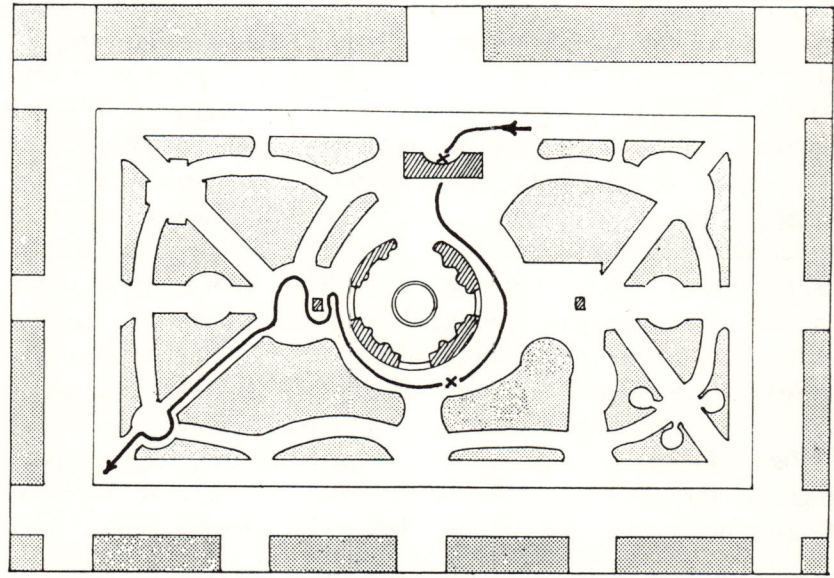

FIGURE 8: Pedestrian Route (a)—two males, black, mid-twenties
(x = listening to pianist; watching juggler)

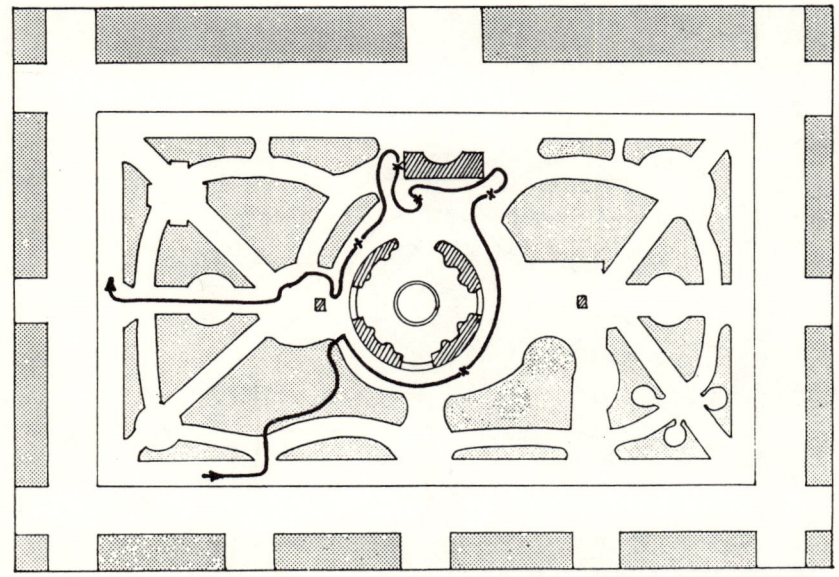

FIGURE 9: Pedestrian Route (b)—two male/female couples, white, mid-twenties
(x = watching juggler; listening to Reggae music; watching Vera; watching comic; listening to jazz)

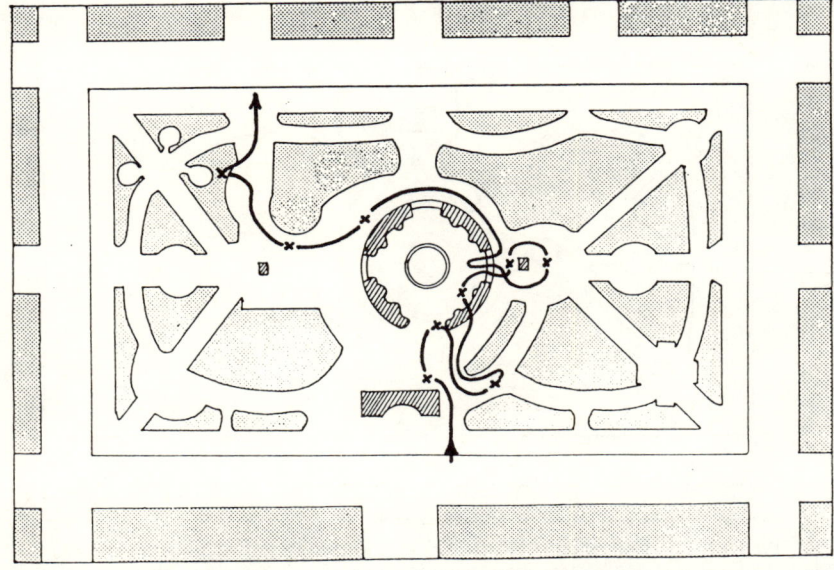

FIGURE 10: Pedestrian Route (c)—two males, white, mid-thirties, in suits
(x = watching Vera; looking into Performance Ring; deciding direction; listening to music; negotiating drug purchase; buying drugs; watching juggler; watching unicyclists; sitting)

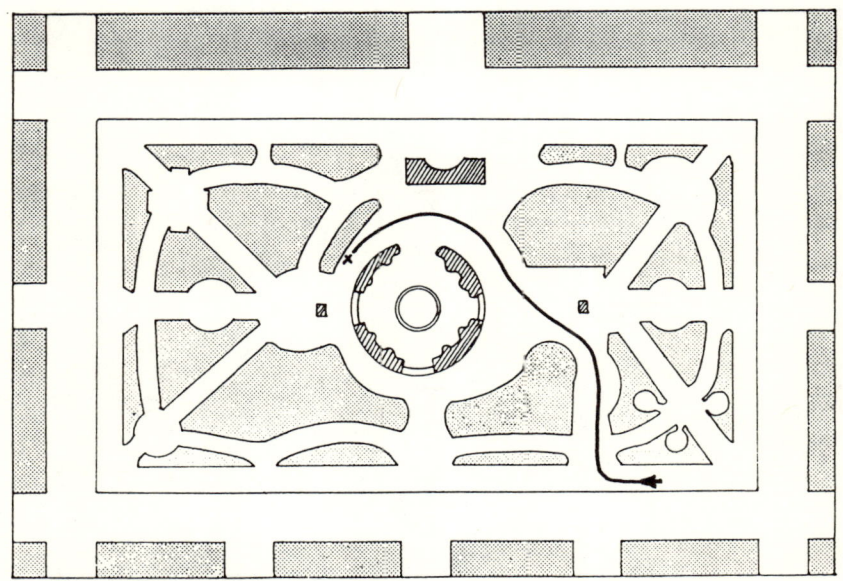

FIGURE 11: Pedestrian Route (d)—two females, white, late sixties
(x = sitting for over one hour)

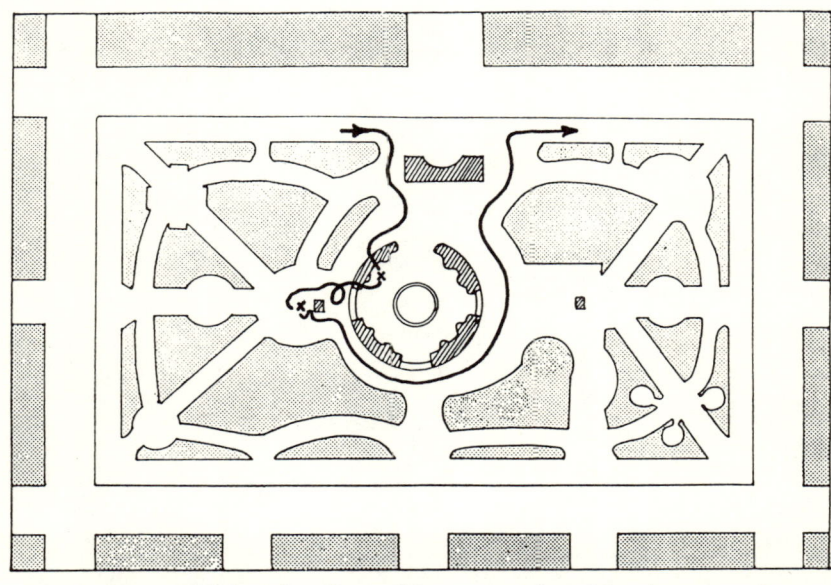

FIGURE 12: Pedestrian Route (e)—one male, white, late twenties
(x = listening to music; buying drugs)

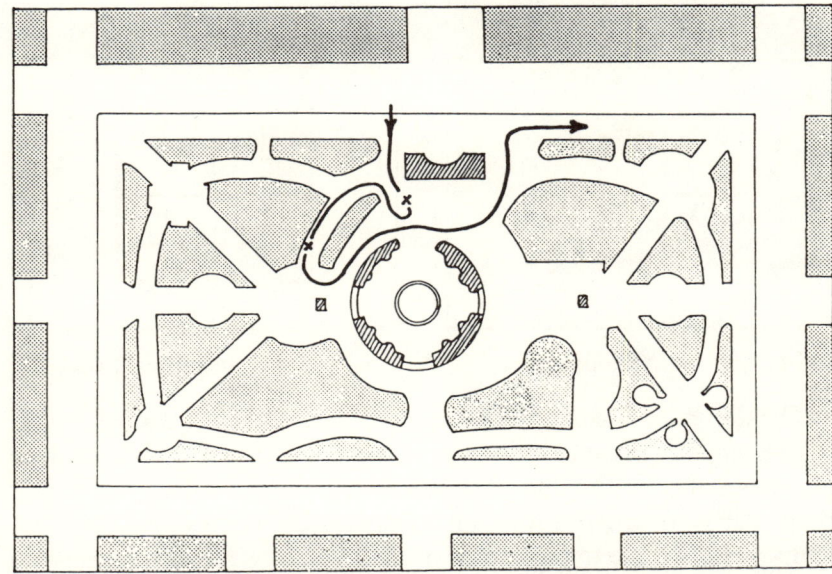

FIGURE 13: Pedestrian Route (f)—one male/female couple with baby, white, early thirties
(x = watching Vera; sitting)

I noticed that several design elements introduced or maintained in the 1970 renovation continue to prompt behaviors that affect street performance. I call these design elements the Star, the Funnel, the Spiral, and the Ring. Each acted as a kind of sieve, allowing the passage of certain behaviors but not others. Each produced a variety of patterns within the square as a whole.

The Star. In *The Hidden Dimension* (1969), Edward T. Hall, citing the 1957 work of Humphrey Osmond, describes two major systems for patterning space: a "sociopetal," or radiating star design, and a "sociofugal," or gridlike arrangement (see Figures 14 and 15).

Hall indicates that these spacial organizations may deeply affect one's perceptions and interactions within them. A sociopetal pattern, for example, is conducive to communication and interaction. People are drawn together through its design as routes merge and overlap. Conversations may ensue. Sociofugal space is more efficient but also more isolating.

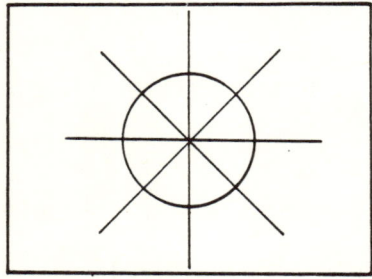 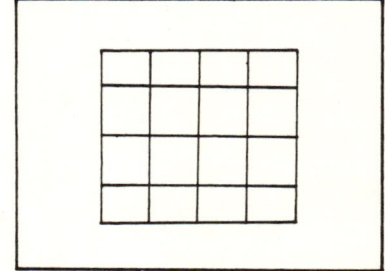

FIGURE 14: Sociopetal Space FIGURE 15: Sociofugal Space

The design of Washington Square, with its spokelike configuration, is an exemplary instance of sociopetal space. People are drawn together via routes that merge and overlap throughout the square. This is a particularly attractive feature of the space. Interviews indicated that many visitors came to the square primarily to interact with others—to meet and talk with friends, watch performers, or establish new friendships. Placing the sociopetal design of Washington Square within the gridlike pattern of New York's streets further enhances our understanding of the square's appeal. In contrast to the environment of the city—with its activities separated and strung out along its streets—Washington Square pulls activities together. Throughout the square, a spontaneous "communitas" emerges—"a direct, immediate and total confrontation of human identities, a deep rather than intense style of personal interaction [that] has something 'magical' about it" (Turner 1982: 47).

The Funnel. The diagonal walkways of this sociopetal space enhance this sense of community, creating a kind of "funnel" into the square and channeling visitors toward the center and the domain of the street performers (see Figure 16). The effect is supported by railings and limited entrances, both of which indicate that the area is set apart from activities outside its boundaries. Persons entering the square sense that it is a special space as they gradually move toward the center, to the Performance Ring.

The Spiral. The curvilinear walkways act as a kind of "spiral" which, despite Olmsted's design principles, intensify rather than pacify the

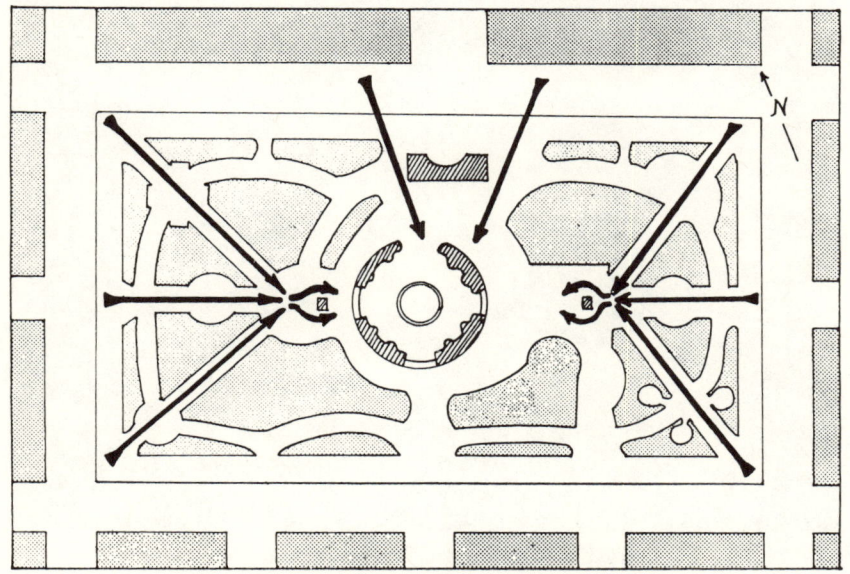

FIGURE 16: The Funnel

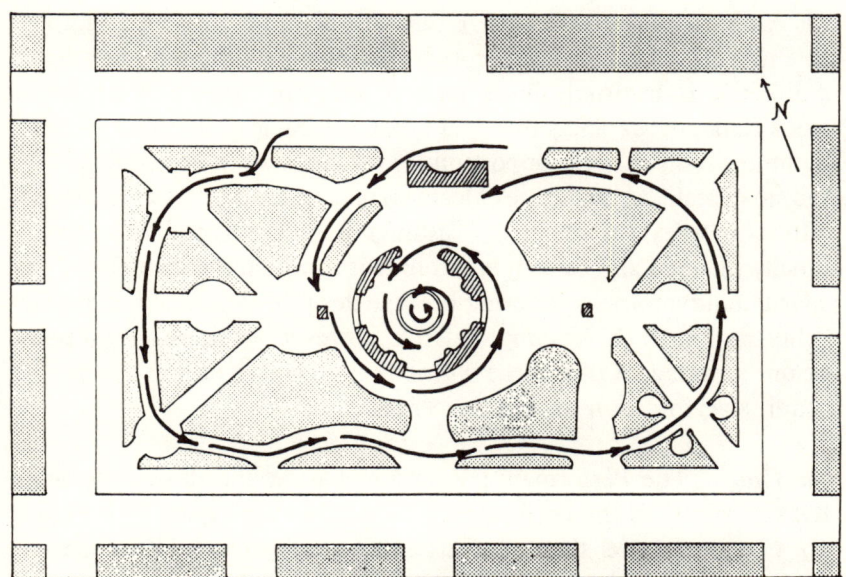

FIGURE 17: The Spiral

Washington Square Walkway, Curved

environment (see Figure 17). Visitors may discover, for example, that it is easier to get into the square than out of it, for it is nearly impossible to walk a straight line through the space. Yet though one's sense of direction is distorted, this is not necessarily an unpleasant sensation. Amos Rapoport explains that "no urban setting is exciting or interesting unless it offers some opportunities for mistakes in orientation. . . . At a small scale, some degree of lostness may be desired" (1977: 207–8).

In some ways, the design of Washington Square resembles an intentionally planned amusement environment in which disorientation, circularity, and aimless wandering become desirable states of being. The eighty-six-foot-high Washington Arch, however, serves as a focal point for one's passage. Confronted with circular choices of movement, the visitor is again drawn toward the center.

The Ring. The Performance Ring also has several design elements that contribute to the performance dynamics of the space (see Figure 18). First, it is lower than the surrounding walkways and thus concentrates activities and people. There are steps into the area on the east, south, and west, and an inclined section of sidewalk descends from the

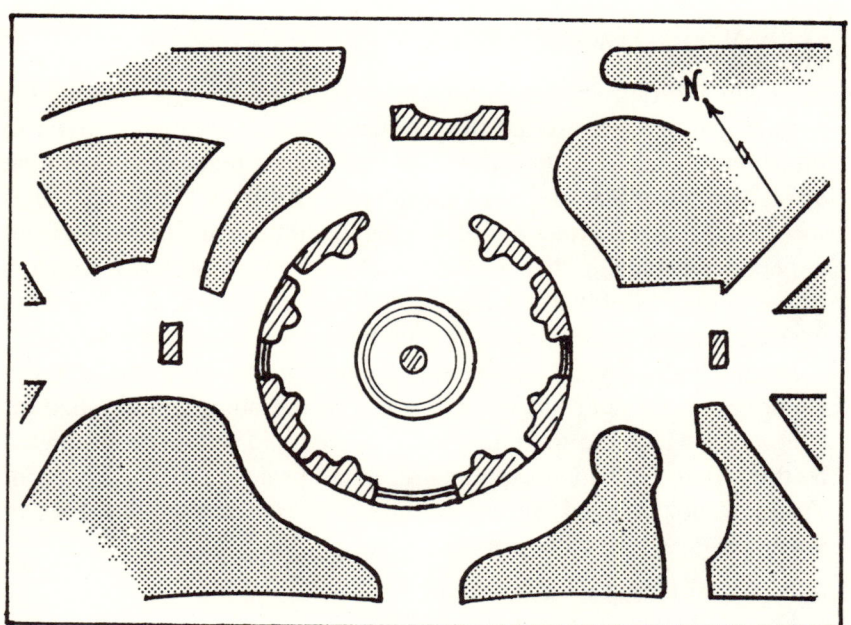

FIGURE 18: The Performance Ring

"Loud Silence as Rebellion"

north. In addition, circular sitting areas, benches facing in toward the fountain, and ledges around the fountain enhance public reflexivity in the square: each person within the ring knows that he or she is on display to all others and acts accordingly. Athletes "perform" their soccer and Frisbee games as well as play them; bizarre individuals wander about, displaying their eccentric behavior to any who will watch; a single woman exhibits "reading a book" and a man practices his banjo in areas so noisy that concentration on the material is certainly doubtful.

Interestingly, several theater theoreticians envisioned similarly dynamic spaces for their indoor performances. Antonin Artaud called for a theater in which the spectator would be engulfed and directly affected by the action. Guillaume Apollinaire, in the prologue to *The Breasts of Tiresias* (1903), called for an environment remarkably like that of Washington Square's Performance Ring:

> A circular theatre with two stages
> One in the middle the other like a ring
> Around the spectators permitting
> The full unfolding of our modern art
> Often connecting in unseen ways as in life
> Sounds gestures colors cries tumults
> Music dancing acrobatics poetry painting
> Choruses action and multiple sets
> (in Benedikt and Wellwarth, 1966: 66)

Schechner, too, often designed his environmental theater performances around a concept that placed the spectator at the center of the action and let the event determine the shape of the theater space.

CONCENTRIC RINGS

The square's active center and the intensities of its surrounding zones of action suggest that the sociopetal design of the square is both centrifugal and centripetal: visitors are both drawn toward and repelled from the central zone. Additionally, the more distant the activities are from the center, the quieter and more self-contained they become. A composite of the square's major activities is mapped on the basis of four concentric rings in Figure 19. Though not as clear-cut as this diagram may imply (the space, unlike the drawing, moves—activities along the diagonal paths especially tend to blur the boundaries), visi-

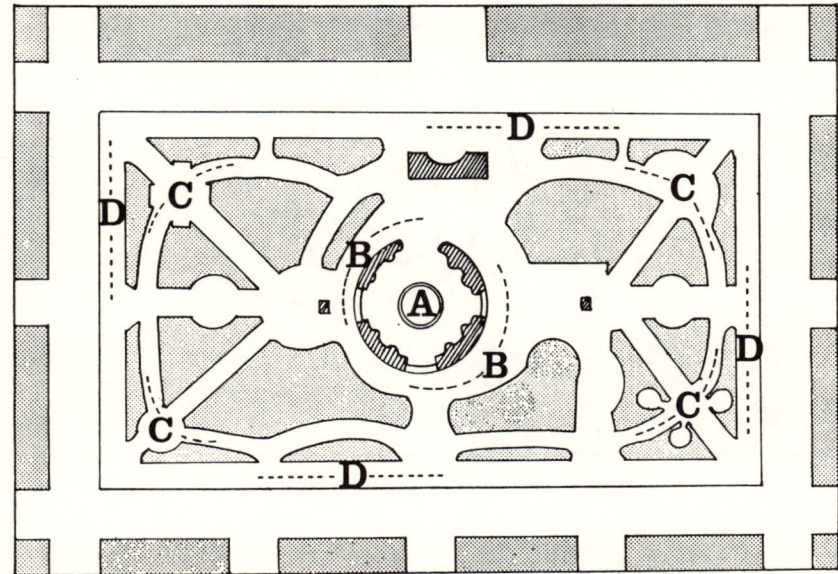

FIGURE 19: Concentric Rings in the Square

tors to the space may nevertheless perceive four major zones of action with decreasing levels of intensity.

Area A is the most "heated" region of the square. Street performers and bizarre exhibitionists are concentrated in this central area. Events move rapidly as acts begin and end; visitors spiral in and out; audiences gather and disperse.

Infrequent or new performers tend to use the more flexible edges of the fixed center in Area B, as do the square's two major "support industries": food vendors and drug dealers. Visitors usually make at least one circuit of this area before entering the center.

Quieter activities featuring fewer participants predominate in Area C. Men play chess at tables in the southwest quadrant; children push one another on swings in one of the playgrounds; couples talk or read in recessed sitting areas. Visitors seeking activities of greater intensity tend to pass through this zone without pausing.

Solo joggers wearing cassette players or radios with earphones move around the square's perimeter in Area D. Pedestrians enter or leave the square from this region. This zone is also used as a "staging ground"

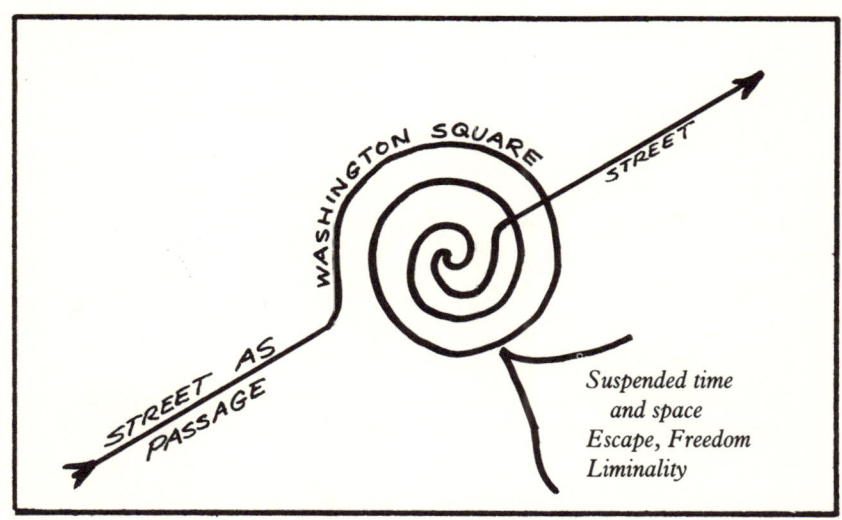

FIGURE 20: The Liminal Space

Aerial View of Washington Square

before entering the square or, alternately, as a place to recollect oneself after a visit.

HOW BEHAVIOR MEANS

The combination of fieldwork and research strategies I have described reveals, in a concrete way, "how behavior means" within a built environment. As Donald Preziosi explains: "In addition to their referential, aesthetic, and allusory functions, architectonic objects also function territorially by staging behavioral routines or episodes, framing interactions, and dividing, structuring, delimiting, or zoning an environment" (1979: 65). Studying movement choices, use patterns, and the amount of time an individual (alone or as part of a group) spends in the setting shows the relationship of the spatial order to the social order. The space's design elements shape the attitudes of its occupants; the space is perceived and defined by the activities one may do in it.

As a result, a mental map may be joined to the physical map of the square. For me, Washington Square becomes a place of suspended time and space, an area chosen for escape or for freedom—perhaps a liminal realm[2] in the midst of New York City (see Figure 20).

As a mirror of its community, Washington Square reflects the pluralism and fluidity of urban life. Often, it brings together people who do not known each other in private or socially intimate spheres and generally do not care to know each other in that way—privacy is a precious and indispensable commodity in New York City. But for several hours on a sunny weekend afternoon, the spontaneous flow of events within its bounds unites people in a powerful feeling of fellowship.

---

2. Victor Turner defines liminality, literally "being-on-a-threshold," as "a state or process which is betwixt-and-between the normal, day-to-day cultural and social states or processes of getting and spending, preserving law and order, and registering structural status. . . . It is a time of enchantment when anything *might*, even should, happen. . . . Liminality is full of potency and potentiality. It may also be full of experiment and play" (in Benamou and Caramello, 1977: 33).

FOUR

Performers in Place

Numerous solo performers and several performance groups visited the square during my documentation period. Those who visited the square infrequently or for only brief periods of time were known as "sideshows" by veteran performers and worked in a "visitors' area." Steve Fogelman, for example, created a popular sideshow attraction in a visitors' area directly west of the arch (Figure 21, #1). For six weeks in 1982, and again in 1984 for most of the summer, Fogelman performed magic and juggling tricks, along with a series of polished acrobatic feats. Audiences were particularly impressed by a finale in which he walked on broken glass. Fogelman said he enjoyed the "risk of the unknown" in street performance and referred to the ways in which a performer has a "direct experience" with an audience's immediate approval or disinterest.

In 1981, an unskilled mime wandered around the square for several weekends (#10). Like Don Littlejohn, the Public Library mime, he would follow people, mimicking their gait and facial expressions for the amusement of people sitting on benches near the Performance Ring. But he was not very good and could not figure out a way to ask for money.

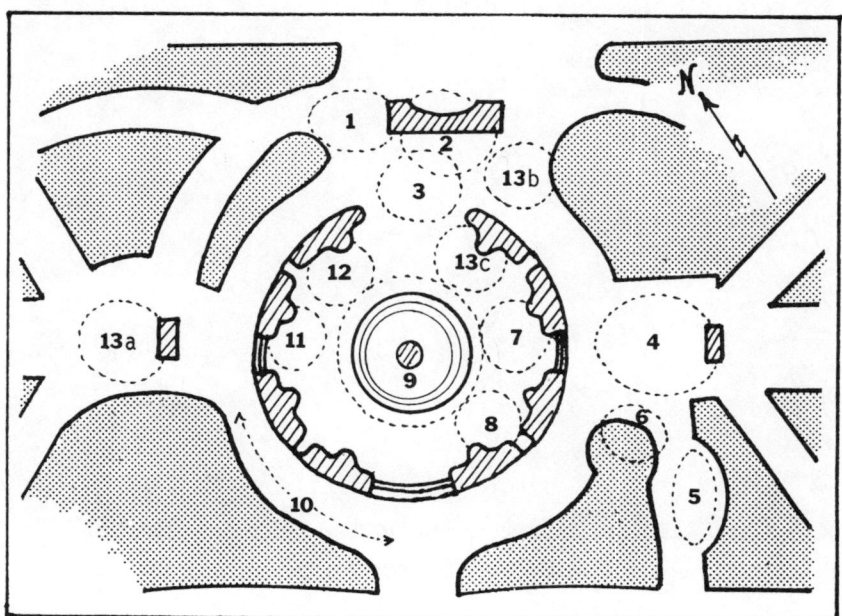

1. Steve Fogelman	6. Blair	11. Jim Gardner
2. Mike Inserra	7. Breakdancers	12. Brewery Puppets
3. Cotton MacAloon	8. Calypso dancer	13a, b, c. Thriller
4. Milo Max	9. Flip Golson	13c. Albert Owens
5. Philippe Petit	10. Timothy Williams	

FIGURE 21: Sideshows and Other Performances, 1981–1984

Tom Mikotowicz and I interviewed him. We learned that Timothy Williams was self-taught and had been performing for three months. His major concerns revolved around his makeup and costumes: "I'm gonna get me some new shoes, and some genie pants. I need to buy some more makeup, and I'm gonna buy some materials for my act. I plan on getting a lot of things. A horn. And I'm gonna get me a cane that turns into a bouquet of flowers, and a friend of mine is gonna teach me a few magic tricks."

Williams returned to the square in 1983. He had added a colorful

Brewery Puppet Troupe

costume and more elaborate makeup, but he still wandered around the square. This time, however, he was waiting for someone to take his picture. As soon as Williams caught a photographer "in the act," he demanded money. This was his entire performance, and Vera told him to leave, at once. I last saw Williams performing in Times Square.

Milo Max, a wandering comedian from Chicago, passed through the square in 1984, performing for a single weekend in front of the Garibaldi statue (#4). Max played a klutzy character who nevertheless managed to perform rather impressive lasso tricks to country-western music, knife juggling to Beethoven's *Ninth Symphony*, and unicycle riding to John Philip Sousa's "Washington Post March"—all while looking absolutely miserable and downtrodden. Audiences were confused, Max grew bitter, and left mid-Sunday.

Philippe Petit worked in the square from time to time, performing his outdoor slack rope routine in an area south of the Garibaldi statue (#5). Twice in 1982, he used Mitchell Cohen's space (#4) to perform with magic and fire torches. He also performed in a media event with Marcel Marceau. Local networks taped the two improvising together in the square and aired their "street performance" on the evening news.

The Brewery Puppet Troupe occasionally performed in Chang's space, which in 1983 and 1984 was also a visitors' area (#12). Using four, three-foot-high puppets resembling crows with movable mouths, the four puppeteers made the crows "sing" to taped Motown and soul music. The operators as well as the puppets danced in the synchronized style of 1970s Motown groups. (Their act reminded me of Bunraku; the operators were visible beneath and around the puppets throughout the show.) They said they preferred to work in Central Park but that Washington Square was good for a "change of pace." They worked outdoors mainly to promote their indoor activities in a Brooklyn church.

Flip Golson, a gymnast from New Haven, Connecticut, visited in 1983 to perform in "Charlie's fountain" (#9). He told me he had heard about Washington Square in New Haven and planned to bring an entire thirty-eight person gymnastic team to perform. But his audience was restless and disinterested—most were waiting for Charlie Barnett to arrive. Golson did not return.

Other performers were invited by Vera as "warm-up" acts for his show. In May 1984, for example, Vera had an "apprentice" (Vera's term) who juggled and performed backflips and balancing tricks. Mike Inserra's act lasted only five minutes and was presented within the chalk circle of Vera's territory (#2). Vera said he was "helping Mike out because he's having a hard time figuring out how to make his act work."

Vera also invited Blair, a magician he met while working the 1983–84 winter season in Key West, Florida. Blair chose the "podium" (#6) to present a fifteen-minute magic show. Blair said afterward that he had selected the space because its railing separated him from the audience. The railing, however, is precisely the reason street performers avoid the space—it is both too isolating and too difficult to pass the hat. Blair said he would try another spot the next afternoon, but he did not return.

Cotton MacAloon, on the other hand, was a talented, energetic, and friendly juggler from Paris, who shared both Vera's and the Millses' locations throughout the summer of 1984 (#3). Not only was his act good, but he also passed several important "rites of entry" by asking Vera where to perform when he first arrived and sharing his beer with the performers.

Cotton MacAloon

In July 1984, Vera enlisted a "partner," a strange older man he called "Swami." Swami's entire routine relied on his ability to catch pigeons. In the middle of a performance, Vera would yell for Swami and ask him to catch a pigeon. Swami would do so, the audience would applaud, and Vera would give him a dollar or two.

Several dance groups also used the square from time to time. On May 27, 1984, for example, a group of twenty teenage dancers known as Thriller performed a choreographed dance piece to Michael Jackson's song of the same title. The group's director, a church drama instructor, heard about the square's spontaneous entertainments and brought the group to perform.

They tried their show in three places. Their first choice, #13a in the "Pharmacy," was clearly a mistake. Drug activity disrupted their show, and they quickly ended the performance, moving to a second location near the arch (#13b). This show attracted a large crowd that suddenly evaporated when Vera purposefully began his act to control the competition. Their third performance choice inside the Performance Ring (#13c) was therefore the best location of the day, given the territoriality and competitiveness of the square.

Numerous breakdancers performed in the space between 1982 and

1984. Most performed in an eastern section of the Performance Ring (#7). One group of six dancers, aged six to fourteen, wore matching yellow tuxedos and used a live drummer. Most groups, however, employed taped music and less elaborate costumes—windbreakers with a name on the back, baseball caps, and basketball shoes were the norm.

One afternoon in June 1984, an exotically dressed African-American man wearing a mask made of peacock feathers danced to calypso music and performed fire-eating tricks in the jazz musicians' space (#8). A woman said she had seen him perform in Central Park.

Another unusual performer worked in the western portion of the Performance Ring (#11) for several months in 1984. At regular intervals throughout the day, Jim Gardner, describing himself as an "escapologist" inspired by Houdini, allowed audience members to place him in a straitjacket, ropes, chains, and padlocks. Gardner would pass the hat via an assistant and then slowly wriggle out of his bondage. He told me, "it's not skill, it's novelty and danger that draws a crowd."

In July 1984, the Manhattan Cable Company brought comedian Albert Owens to the square to make a video on street performers. (The crew could not tell me why their company chose Owens over performers who actually worked in Washington Square.) Owens began his act by announcing: "I am not Charlie. I am Albert." Evidently, he hoped to use Barnett's notoriety as a device to promote his own act, even though he performed in the northeast quadrant of the Performance Ring (#13c) rather than in Barnett's area. As the crew began taping the show, a police officer arrived and told Owens he could not use a microphone. Owens refused to perform without it, remarking to the crowd: "You can't do anything here, man. Why'd they put this place here?" The audience, however, urged Owens to continue the show anyway and refused to leave. "Charlie never used a mike," someone yelled.

Here was an opportunity for the Manhattan Cable Company to use the officer's entrance as part of the tape and film the audience's response. Certainly this is a fundamental part of outdoor performances in New York City. But the crew simply decided to tape the act somewhere else. They packed up and left, and the video became only an outdoor "indoor performance," rather than a documentation of what really happens when a performer works on New York's sidewalks.

THE MAIN ATTRACTIONS

We now turn to a more detailed discussion of four of the square's major performers. Each of these performers worked in the square for a year or more during my documentation period. Each maintained a clearly defined territory within or directly adjacent to the Performance Ring. These performers also created a unique (yet coincidental) diversity in the square: Chang was Vietnamese; Steve and Carol Mills typified white middle America; Mitchell Cohen was a fifty-year-old native New Yorker; Charlie Barnett was an African-American hustler from Boston. I documented each of their shows regularly and interviewed each performer on several occasions.

Chang. In April 1981, two jugglers, Nguyen Phuc and Paul Bonnien, performed in the open space west of the fountain. The performers were new, not only to the square but also to street performing. Their act was silent and nonparticipative—they simply juggled, barely acknowledging the audience, and then passed the hat. Asked about their location, Phuc said he was uncomfortable with the full arena of the Performance Ring and preferred to use Holly Plaza's statue as a backdrop.

Phuc and Bonnien worked irregularly. In one interview, Phuc claimed he was working his way through school, using the money from street performing to earn an M.B.A. at Fordham University. In a later interview, however, Phuc had forgotten our earlier discussion and denied being anything other than a street performer.

In June 1982, Phuc received a nickname from Vera—"Chang"—and began to work alone in the Performance Ring. His act changed rapidly, not only because he was working without Bonnien but also because he was learning the important patter, flair, and pacing of a street text. He started explaining his routines by adding funny names or histories. He asked the audience to chant or clap in rhythm during his routines. Already a skilled juggler, able to juggle up to seven objects simultaneously, Chang was absorbing more fundamental street strategies concerning the necessity for dialogue and participation. As one juggler explained: "People don't care about tricks unless you make them care somehow" (in Campbell, 1981: 99).

Chang Juggling in Holly Plaza

Most of Chang's material was not original; it was "borrowed" from several well-known performers in Washington Square or nearby spots. He added, for example, a common street juggling routine in which, while juggling five balls, a performer asks, "Want to see six?" When the audience inevitably responds affirmatively, the performer holds up six balls and lays them down again. Preparing to light his fire torches, Chang asked, "Anybody here have a lighter? Will you throw that to me?" Then, "Okay, anybody here have a gold watch?" Following a particularly difficult technique, he would quip, "Want to see that again? Come back tomorrow." At the end of his show, he would remark, "One of the nicest things about street performing is that you always get a standing ovation." All of these comic bits were part of acts elsewhere in the square or on nearby Sixth Avenue.

Chang began to claim he had been performing in Washington Square for four years, thus identifying endurance and commitment as useful codes of outdoor entertaining. He drew on his Asian background as a central, organizing aesthetic for his performance. Though actually from

Vietnam, he told his audience he was from China (perhaps not wishing to add stressful memories to his audience's perception of the act). He donned a black kung-fu uniform with a yellow sash and an embroidered dragon on the back and added fluid, martial arts–style movements to his routines.

In August 1982, Chang shared Vera's performing territory directly south of Washington Arch, announcing, "Tony's show is starting soon, this is a warm-up." Each weekend, Vera and several visiting performers watched Chang's show and offered advice: "You gotta speed that part up or it won't be funny"; "That's not working, why not get rid of it?"; "That's really good. You should put it sooner in the show." Chang was beginning the process of revision, refinement, and personalizing which creates a unique street act.

He began to introduce his show as follows:

> Today, ladies and gentlemen, all the way from China, I have for you a demonstration of the Chinese Devil Stick. It was invented by Mr. Ching Wah Wah many thousands of years ago. The stick will rise up into the air to defy Newton's law. It is mind over matter—and even if you don't mind, it doesn't matter. The trick is from China. The stick is from New Jersey.
>
> And this is a live show. So, when I do a good trick I would like all of you to clap your hands real loud, okay? This is a two-way communication. It's not like TV, you know, when you stay home and watch.
>
> And now I would like all of you to clap your hands and yell real loud. Then all the people will rush over to see the show. And the more people we have, the more money—I mean, the more *fun*—we'll have.

Chang would then demonstrate several variations of Devil Stick juggling: "Chopsticks," "Over the Shang Hai Bridge," "Behind the Bamboo Tree," "Under the Bridge," and, intentionally dropping the stick, "In the Water." "Sometimes I have to drop it in order to make it look difficult," he would remark as part of the show. Later, he would perform "samurai" and "kung-fu" juggling techniques that relied on leg kicks, hand chops, and martial arts yells.

Other routines presented a foreigner's view of America: the "Tax Collector," "New York Staying Alive," "Ronald Reagan Balanced

Budget," and "Disco" juggling routines. He also told his audience that when he first came to this country he moved to New York and decided to learn English. "So I locked myself in a room and watched television for three months. Then I realized it was a Spanish station. Only in New York!"

Chang's finale and pitch included a complicated and well-choreographed routine with fire torches, kicks, and an acrobatic split on the pavement. He began by announcing:

> And now, from five different countries, I have for you a big combination. Between the legs, behind the back, the Belgian kick-out and the French—it's a very long trick. To save time, I'll just show you the ending. (He assumes a dramatic stance and holds up the torches.) Hey!
>
> Yeah, you New Yorkers always want to see the whole thing. So here we go. The whole routine. (He presents the long and complex routine. At its conclusion, he again assumes the earlier dramatic stance and shouts:) Hey! (Audience applauds.) Thank you very much.
>
> One of the nicest things about street performing is that you always get a standing ovation. And here's your chance to become a patron of the arts, to support street theater in New York City and save yourself a trip to San Francisco. Thank you also for supporting my wife and thirteen kids. Thank you very much. Stay where you are, I'll come and collect.

Washington Square audiences enjoyed Chang's show. Other performers, however, said that Chang never really "owned" his performance. He borrowed his routines, a strategy that is acceptable only for novices. Veteran street performers insist that more experienced performers must develop their own material through their show's unique relationship to its environment and its audiences. Chang never achieved this level of performance, instead offering a show that varied in only minor ways. He recited most of his jokes regardless of logical motivation or audience setup. Vera, however, said he "gave" a spot to Chang because "it's good to have an exotic person around—it gives the square some class, some atmosphere."

I later learned that Chang lived in Philadelphia and was pursuing several indoor performance options, including a job on a Caribbean

Steve and Carol Mills Juggle Fire on Unicycles

cruise ship. Off the streets, he began to perform as "Thien Fu." In 1984, Nguyen Phuc/Chang/Thien Fu left the square for good. Vera said Chang was working for Ringling Brothers/Barnum and Bailey—a dream job for many street jugglers. Though it was always difficult to unearth the truth of Chang's contradictory stories about himself and his life, this too illustrates a part of the street performer's role and personality: the performer as dreamer, fabricator, and unconventional rebel.

Steve and Carol Mills. The Millses met at a 1977 jugglers' convention in Delaware, when Steve was twenty and Carol was seventeen. A year later, they married and formed their act. "We thought about it for a while," Steve said, "and decided to call ourselves Steve and Carol." Because Carol was new to street performing, Steve took charge of the patter in their outdoor unicycle, juggling, and comedy act. Carol was the only female street performer I encountered in New York, and she had never worked alone.

During the summer of 1979, the Millses performed in Sheridan Square on Seventh Avenue in Greenwich Village, commuting from Steve's parents' home in Morristown, New Jersey. They traveled with their act during the winter, one year as far as New Zealand, and also gave performances for local elementary schools. One year, they did a halftime show for the Harlem Globetrotters. "But during the summers," Steve explained, "we like to stay in one place." "We consider street performing our vacation," Carol added, "'cause it's nicer out here."

I asked Carol if they were professional performers. Carol hesitated so I asked her to tell me what she thought a professional performer was. "Somebody who likes what they're doing and makes people happy," she said. Steve added, "An amateur is somebody who enjoys what they're doing, but a professional is somebody who makes money at it. An amateur means you're just doing it for the love of it, whether you're getting paid or not. We really love it, but we also do it for a living." In a later interview, the Millses returned to my question, telling me they had thought about it and decided that the difference between professional and amateur performers concerned how "polished" a performer was allowed to be: "Indoors, polish is everything. Outside though, we don't get as much money if we're too good." They concluded that, because outdoor economics prevents performers from being too polished, street performers cannot be professionals in the fullest sense of the word.

The Millses began to perform in Washington Square in 1981. They tried several spots in the square, moving from the sidewalk south of the Performance Ring to the eastern roller skaters' area to a location near Vera and the arch. They mentioned the "right karma" for a spot and stressed the importance of respecting another performer's location, noting, "We won't perform while Tony's doing a show. . . . It's a mean thing to do."

"A lot of times you'll get an idiot, an outsider, who doesn't know how, you know, the performers here treat one another," Carol said.

"Yeah, but it'd only be a one-night thing," Steve remarked. "Most performers find out how it's done before they start performing somewhere."

They added that street performing requires cooperation to avoid arrest. "As long as no one complains, as long as we're all cool, then we can perform 'cause we're not hurting anybody. . . . If somebody complains, *then* it's against the law."

They arranged for their location near Washington Arch by offering to trade shows with Vera, pointing out that the arrangement would keep audiences in the area for longer periods of time. They usually arrived around 12:00 noon and at first performed only on Sundays.

Carol explained: "The tourists are here between 12:00 and 4:00 P.M., and we get more money from the tourists." In 1982, however, they began to work on Saturdays as well. They also adopted new navy blue T-shirts with "The Dazzling Duo" inscribed on the front. "During daytime shows we used to wear all black," Carol said, "but Tony wears black, so we've changed it." "Besides, everybody can see us up on our unicycles," Steve added, "so it really doesn't matter so much."

Each time audiences left Vera's show, Steve would yell, "Show time! Show time over here, folks!" to capture the exiting crowd's attention. He usually began the show alone, working with juggling clubs and fire torches. Responding to scattered applause, Steve would yell, "Wait! Wait! I'm just warming up!" He would then ask the audience to yell and applaud as loudly as possible, explaining: "The more yelling, the more people. And the more people, the more money—I mean *fun*—we'll have!" Steve claimed that he created this routine, as well as Chang's lines about street performers receiving a standing ovation and his "Want to see that again? Come back tomorrow" quip. (Comedian Barnett also used the initial, audience-gathering strategy, but possibly he borrowed it from the Millses as well, since both performed in Sheridan Square in 1981. Such lines of transmission are difficult to trace, however.)

Following the crowd-gathering routine, Steve and then Carol mounted their six-foot unicycles to begin an increasingly complex series of routines: jumping rope, juggling clubs behind their backs ("Remember, this is for *your* entertainment. I've seen it before"), and passing fire torches ("We're going to throw these things at each other's face—just for *your* amusement!"). Steve talked continuously, using a series of smooth one-liners in response to remarks from the audience. Steve announced, for example: "We'd like to take a moment to introduce ourselves." Then he and Carol would solemnly shake hands with each other.

Carol's role was that of the "inept female," unable to mount her bike, catch the torches, or pay attention. Toward the end of the show, Steve would convince a woman in the audience to sit on his shoulders as he careened around the circle on his unicycle, yelling to Carol, "See, *she's* stupid enough to do this!"

The Millses had many regular fans, some of whom were jugglers themselves. Ned, of the former Washington Square juggling team Ned and Will, said that Steve and Carol had the smoothest routines he had seen in years. Their energy was so focused that even regulars laughed at the same jokes from show to show.

After about twenty minutes, the Millses approached the moment of their pitch. Steve teased the audience, saying: "And now, at last, the amazing trick!—You might have *heard* about this next trick. You might have *read* about it. . . . Probably neither." Steve would stress the dangers and difficulties of the stunt. He would request quiet, rearrange the front row of spectators, and generally drag the finale out as long as possible. Finally, Carol would hand him three lit torches, and, putting on a felt hat to protect his hair, he would ride his unicycle around the circle while juggling the torches under his legs. It was a difficult and impressive feat.

Following a burst of enthusiastic applause, Steve would bow and announce from his six-foot perch: "Before you go, I have two things to say to you. First, you've been a great audience. Second, remember that last movie you went to see? It was *lousy!* You paid *five bucks* to see it! You were burned! Well, today, ladies and gentlemen, Carol and I have given you a bargain." Leaping down from his unicycle, Steve would remove his hat and begin to circle the crowd. Carol would circle from the other side. The majority of contributions in their hats were dollar bills, netting about fifty dollars a show.

Mitchell Cohen. Mitchell Cohen, a former Madison Avenue advertising agency writer in his mid-fifties, raced turtles in Washington Square, using an elaborate set, real turtles with funny names and numbers on their backs, and an eloquent verbal routine relying on a comic inversion of horse racing. He began the race as a hobby, performing at the Charles Street fair in Greenwich Village for nearly ten years as part of his "civic duty." "Initially, I approached it like a game with some funny commentary. I even allowed myself to pay vendor's fees at the fairs the first couple of years. Then someone said, 'Hey, this is entertainment!' A very unusual entertainment, but entertainment."

As the material improved and as audiences laughed harder and longer, it became an increasingly attractive alternative to his Madison Avenue job. "I'd always felt that I'd like to be one of those who's kind

Mitchell Cohen: "Post Time!"

of symbolic of the fun that can just sort of serendipitously happen on a nice warm spring day," Cohen explained. "That makes me feel good." He described his act as a "vehicle that makes some satirical comments on America's reverence for muscle and skill and athletic prowess at the expense of all else." "It always rankled me somehow," Cohen said, "that the second violinist of the New York Philharmonic makes about 10 percent of what the average rookie baseball player makes during his first year with the New York Mets."

In 1982, Cohen abandoned his weekday job and became a full-time street performer. He tried the Public Library but felt he was an "intrusion." He moved to the Metropolitan Museum and found it too noisy. On Wall Street, the audience was the problem: "Boy are they dull! They just stand around saying 'duh. . . .' And they've got gangrene of the knuckles" (meaning they don't contribute money).

In March 1983, Vera saw Cohen and his turtles performing on Sixth Avenue and invited him to the square. Asked if he had been "assigned" his performance space near the Garibaldi statue, Cohen responded: "I have a lot of respect for Tony. . . . He invited me, and we came to a mutual understanding about where I wanted to work and where I could work."

The turtles performed on a "handy dandy break-down do-it-yourself portable Turtle Drome"—basically, a hexagonal stage on legs. "A couple years ago," Cohen said, "I got astroturf! Boy was that exciting. You know, each little addition, to me, is like some Greek shipowner getting a new ship. And I save things for special occasions—little 'turtle hurdles,' a wind-up turtle truck, and a big orange turtle with wobbly eyes I call Franken Turtle."

The act began with Cohen shouting, in a voice somewhere between that of a carnival pitchman and a racetrack announcer:

> Step up! Step up, everyone! The turtles are on the track! These are great thoroughbred racing turtles, come from far away to be with you this afternoon.
> Come forward everyone. Come on up—especially you, my dear. Step up, step up everyone.
> Right now, they're doing their wind sprints, their setting-up exercises, getting loose, getting limber. Anything to break the tension that always accompanies the running of a major event.

Drawing the curious toward his turtle-racing arena, Cohen would announce that the day's race was the "feature race of the afternoon," "the famed Twin Tiara," or the "Washington Square Futility," thereby establishing the satiric basis of the act.

Next, Cohen introduced the turtles, asking the audience to "give each turtle a warm round of applause"—the first participatory gesture of the show. In 1983, the turtles were the transsexual Lana Turtle, formerly known as Engelburt Hump, who entered the race during the time Renee Richards, the transsexual tennis player, was in the news; Slimo Greeno, who Cohen said corresponded to baseball's Hank Aaron, "with more victories lifetime than any turtle now competing"; Maximillian Shell, returning from "near-fatal" knee surgery, but making a spectacular comeback as "1983's Reptile of the Year"; Sublime Shalimar, "formerly the jewel of the Shah's stable, she is today a political exile—banished by the Aya Turtle"; and Ivan the Terrapin, the first professional racing turtle to defect from the Soviet Union. The race's winner, Cohen explained, pointing to his "official" T-shirt, would be declared under the rules of the "New York State Turtle Racing Authority, Joseph T. Noonan, Commissioner." He would inform the audience that they could bet on the turtles for free, remarking, "This is my contribution to your afternoon's exposure to cultural events. If your turtle wins, you'll receive a prize that is guaranteed absolutely worthless!"

Cohen would move around the circle, asking people to call out their bets. Some called out bets immediately. Others simply watched. Cohen would move toward the less participative spectators, threatening to *assign* them a turtle if they refused to bet voluntarily. He often spent nearly five minutes on this segment, believing that selecting a turtle is "a very bonding moment in the act."

Originally, the turtles were numbered sequentially from one to five, with little plastic numerals stuck on their backs each morning. One weekend, however, Cohen ran out of a numeral two so he numbered the turtles from one to six with the two left out. During the betting, however, someone called out "Number Two." Cohen responded, "Oh, Number Two's been scratched due to a drug inquiry." This quick retort was met with such laughter that the faulty numbering remained in the act to prompt one of a series of quips Cohen called his "canned ripostes."

"I would like to say a word about why I'm doing this," Cohen would then announce. By this point, the absurdity of the situation was so well defined that this simple statement met with another burst of laughter. "We're trying to build a new wing at the St. Elmo's Home for Retired Racing Turtles in Galapagos, New Mexico. . . . Folks, those retired racing superstars need everything! They need little turtleneck sweaters to guard them against the chill night air; and they need Shell . . . *Oil!*; and Turtle . . . *Wax!*" Cohen would reveal the back of the "1983 Poster Turtle," advising those "close to the emotional borderline" not to look. "But for the rest, especially you old-time sports fans, I'm sure you'll remember him with a tear in your eye: Old Number Fourteen, Mr. Y. A. Turtle!" The name was a pun on the retired New York Giants quarterback, Y. A. Tittle. The poster featured a sketch of a bandaged turtle sitting in an armchair.

Next, Cohen asked for a volunteer from the audience, stipulating that the volunteer be male, courageous, and strong. Following a brief pause, he would drag a man out of the audience who generally did not

Cohen's Volunteer

quite fit the description. Cohen told me he looked for "an executive type. . . . someone who'll be a good sport and won't take the focus off the act." Cohen convinced his volunteer to wear a silly rubber finger puppet and a brass "helmet." The volunteer was also given an aluminum pot-lid "shield." If a turtle became motionless during the race, Cohen would explain, the volunteer was to lean over the rail and, "at great peril to your upper torso," wag his finger puppet at the turtle while yelling "'Wooga Wooga!' in a great commanding voice." (Actually, the stunt never made any difference, but the audience enjoyed the volunteer's foolishness.)

Once, Cohen said, he made a serious error in judgment:

> I inadvertently picked a Hell's Angel. He wasn't wearing the jacket, but as he got into the circle, I realized he was the size of a mountain, he had studded wristbands, tattoos—you know, the works. I tentatively offered the helmet. He wouldn't wear it. He wouldn't wear the

helmet, he wouldn't carry the shield, he wouldn't do anything. So, you know what I did? I said "You're fired." And I got out of it! He walked away, and I did it without an assistant.

Usually, however, once the volunteer was successfully selected and instructed, Cohen would take out a trumpet-shaped kazoo and begin to play part of the familiar racetrack melody. Stopping abruptly—"Well, you know how it goes"—he would abandon the kazoo and place the turtles behind a "central barricade" (a plastic set of folding walls), announcing "It's post time! The turtles are pawing the turf—ready to begin their run to glory! When this barricade is raised, the turtles will *explode* from the gate! [scattered laughter] You're going to have to take this more seriously, sir, [pointing to a quiet section of the audience] like those people over there."

"Are you ready?" Cohen then asked the volunteer, who would nod, laughing. "Try to get control of yourself, man. This is dangerous work." Cohen would grab a wind-up toy of a boy riding a bicycle, announcing: "The field is in the hands of the Central Starter!" Winding up the toy and letting it go, Cohen would raise the barricade. The turtles walked slowly toward the walls of the set, the audience cheering and laughing, the volunteer waving his finger puppet and shouting "Wooga Wooga," while Cohen, adopting the tone of a racetrack announcer, droned "and moving up on the outside, it's Number Five, Sublime Shalimar. As they round the Clubhouse Turn, here comes Number One."

Finally, one of the turtles would meander across the finish line. Cohen, grabbing a large checkered flag and waving it high in the air, would yell "And it's Number Six, ladies and gentlemen. Number Six, Ivan the Terrapin!" Placing number six in the center of the track, he would award the victorious turtle a tiny eucalyptus wreath. The audience would cheer and applaud.

At this point, Cohen began the least successful segment of his act. Rather than immediately converting the audience's enthusiasm and participation into a profitable pitch, Cohen—for reasons I could not identify—preferred to try to hold the audience's attention for one more comic routine: the awards ceremony for the winners in the audience. As spectators drifted away, satisfied by the race, Cohen's voice would

Racing to the Finish Line

begin to rise: "Wait. Who had Number Six? You lucky devils. You are going to receive replicas, in living fake cheap stuff, of the greatest racing turtle of all time! Ladies and gentlemen, a turtle of the people. The great Egyptian champion—Turtle Kamen!" The crowd would groan at the pun, wandering away as Cohen handed out small plastic turtles to the winners, shouting, "Okay, that's the show, ladies and gentlemen. I hope you enjoyed it, and I do hope you remember those retired racing superstars at the St. Elmo's Home. You've been a terrific audience, *so far!*" He would move around the departing audience with his hat. "You're losing ground!" He would continue until all had left.

The pitch was clearly a major problem in Cohen's act. I asked him how he felt about the act's ending and asking for money. Cohen replied:

> Well, I'm a middle-class guy. I was brought up as a middle-class kid, and it's not really my style to pass the hat. Yet circumstances have kind of dictated that instead of integrating it into the act [as a contribution before the race, which might be misinterpreted as a bet], I now pass the hat.

> I feel that what I've put out is really top-quality entertainment, and that I *deserve* rewards. Yet all of us [street performers] are constantly bucking the axiom that what you get for nothing is of little value.

Cohen had said during the show, however, that it was "free" to bet on the turtles and that the performance was his "contribution to [their] afternoon's cultural exposure." Each of these phrases could indicate to someone unfamiliar with the economic pressures of street performing that it was, in fact, a free show—Cohen emphasized *his* contribution rather than theirs. It seemed as if, because he felt guilty about passing the hat, he tried to emphasize other reasons for doing the show. He once said, for example:

> It's like I'm out here putting notes in bottles. In a way, the turtle races are a window into me. Anybody with perception will recognize that this is only the tip of my creative iceberg, and hopefully someone will find me who can utilize my imagination. The really perceptive ones are the ones who come up to me afterward and ask 'What else do you do?'"

In June 1983, he said:

> It takes a certain kind of person, a certain toughness, to perform out on the street. And I wonder, and I'm just speaking for myself, is it toughness, or desperation? There are some people who are best doing what they do, and *this* is what I *do*. But you know, I might do more if I wasn't such a coward. Of course, there's the argument that the bravest ones are the cowards who do it anyway, but I don't know. Yeah, sometimes I feel like a soldier on a mission. I walk into Washington Square Park and I never know if this is going to be my last day here.

Cohen ceased performances in July 1983, having negotiated a series of paid performances at Battery Park and in F. A. O. Schwartz's toy store on Fifth Avenue.

Charlie Barnett. Charlie Barnett was the square's most notorious street performer. He was primarily a stand-up comedian; his routines were legendary among regular visitors, and his antics were a frequent topic of conversation among performers as well. Barnett generally

Charlie Barnett Prepares His Audience

worked Saturday evenings, though he occasionally gave late afternoon shows on Sundays. His schedule was irregular and the length of each performance unpredictable. One show might last over an hour, the next only fifteen minutes. Each show seemed to depend upon a unique combination of Barnett's and his audience's shifting moods.

Barnett was the only performer who had the courage, or at least the physical stamina, to perform in the natural amphitheater of the dry fountain, usually a curiously void space in the midst of great activity. Its steplike ledges provided seating for three hundred or more spectators, and a raised metal disk in the center provided a platform from which Barnett delivered his opening remarks. The fixed seating controlled his huge audiences, while the circular arrangement directed the crowd's attention to Barnett. Most Saturday evenings, I would find fifty or more fans gathered near the fountain "waiting for Charlie." Often, Barnett lingered in the center. "Yeah, that's him," they would say. "That's Charlie." "How long, Charlie?" someone would shout. He would glance over at Vera's act. "Two minutes."

Like the Millses, Barnett began his show just as Vera's audience dispersed. Standing on one of the ledges surrounding the fountain, he would yell, "It's show time! Next show starting now! Okay everyone, over here!" Another fifty or so spectators would join those already around the fountain's ledge. Barnett would then announce: "I've got a *terrific* show for you tonight, but I'm not going to do it for less than *half* the square's population!" In the past, Barnett enticed the crowd with a few jokes; more recently, however, he reminded them of their role in his introductory routine: "Y'all know me and my show, and y'all know what to do. So when I count to three, everybody's gonna yell, cheer, applaud, whistle, scream, and make so much racket that everybody else'll think I'm getting killed over here and they'll come to watch!" The yelling usually ended in a chant: "Charlie . . . Charlie. . . Charlie. . ." as Barnett swaggered around the ring. As the show progressed, he would fling himself around the center, strutting, dancing, rapping, smoking and absorbing his power from the crowd. Though his attitude became increasingly superior and intimidating, his energy held the spectators' attention throughout the performance.

Barnett's humor was topical and specific to New York City. Introducing himself, he would say, "My name is Charlie Barnett. I live in Harlem, but I've got a summer home in Newark," hinting at a New Yorker's idea of the two worst places one could live in the area. "One thing I like about New York," he would say. "Everybody has the same fuckin' name—'Yo!'" "Yeah, we can always spot you tourists, too. You guys look at stuff we don't give a fuck about anymore. 'Oh look, Myrtle, the Washington Arch.' Who cares, right?"

Unlike Cohen's material, Barnett's routines relied on stylized rudeness and a series of rapidly delivered insults, usually based on stereotypical prejudices. He insulted everyone—African-American, gay, Upper East Side, tourists, Puerto Ricans—with carefree enthusiasm. "I do a lot of ethnic humor," he would remark, "and people ask me if I'm prejudiced. Well, let me be honest with you all: I'm not black! This is a *birthmark!* . . . But really, I do *everybody*—'cause what interests me is how everyone does stuff different." Often, while imitating one group, he would say, "Don't worry, I'm gonna do blacks." He would imitate his victims' behavior on the streets (imitating homosexuals was a favorite) or in the bedroom (demonstrating, for example, the lovemaking styles of Asian, Jewish, or southern women). He would point to representatives from the parodied group and ask, "Isn't that right?" They would respond with giggles and embarrassment.

The pace of his performance reflected the tempo and pressure of its urban existence. He used gestures, postures, walks, leaps, and a shouted delivery "constantly breaking into hostile absurdity and forcing audiences to laugh, maybe a little harder than they would like to, about the desperateness of their own lives" (Smith, 1981: 15). The playfulness of the square's overall environment, combined with Barnett's and the majority of his audience's enthusiasm, managed to reframe and manipulate the context of Barnett's abuse.

His act was less structured than the other performers'. Barnett seemed to choose routines as they occurred to him. Regular fans knew much of Barnett's material by heart. Often, someone would call out: "Charlie, do the exorcist joke," or "Hey, tell us about the pope." One popular segment concerned the large transistor radios black adolescents carried on the streets and subways: "White folks hate it when niggers get on the cars with them goddam radios. Honkies just get mad as shit. And niggers don't get on with no itty bitty boxes. When they get on the train, everybody's gotta wait for them to put the speakers up in the corners!"

Barnett would locate a white man in the audience who was wearing a tie and perhaps a jacket and, pulling him into the circle, would announce: "Okay, listen. This is your chance to get us niggers back. I'm gonna be you. And *you* can be *me*" (raised eyebrow glance to the audience). He would borrow the man's coat and tie (on one occasion, Barnett even took the man's briefcase and an expensive pen) while convincing his volunteer/accomplice to wear a backward baseball cap, roll up one pants leg, and carry a large radio borrowed from another audience member.

"Okay, I'm on the train. It's 5:00, I've had a hard day at the office, and I'm trying to read my *Wall Street Journal* [another prop taken from the audience]. Then you get on the car."

His volunteer often needed coaching—"Don't you know how to turn that radio on?" "No, niggers don't walk like that. It's like this." Finally, the man would enter the scene. Soon, he would be strutting around the imaginary subway car, relishing the opportunity to turn up the volume and wave the radio in Barnett's face. Barnett would look up and say, in a prissy voice, "*Will* you turn that thing off!" The audience would break into laughter and applause at the spontaneous "psychodrama" taking place before their eyes. The man would try to be even more obnoxious until actors and audience were laughing so hard the skit broke apart.

Joyfully abusive of everyone in his audience, Barnett would ridicule their clothing, lover, job, apartment—whatever he suspected was important to his quarry. "A lot of people say I'm offensive," he would remark, "but I don't give a fuck!" He would imitate the way different groups go to work (the Polish walk backward, Asians take tiny steps, African-Americans saunter down the street muttering, "I should get there by payday") He would mimic a tourist encountering an African-American New Yorker ("Will you mug me, while my husband takes a picture?"), discuss African-American teenager fashions ("If you were a cab driver, would *you* pick this person up?" pointing to someone in the audience), and the way Puerto Ricans lend money ("Okay, you see this knife? You see my thumb?" *Chop*. "Yeah, I just cut off my thumb, so you *know* I don't give a shit about your head!"). Audiences would laugh at these recognizable distillations of daily life. He would twist his face into a caricature of a Japanese tourist discovering the World Trade Center towers. Moving around the circle with tiny steps, holding an imaginary camera around his neck ("You don't never see a Jap without a camera"), he peppered the audience with a complex combination of prejudices, truths, and fantasies, all propelled by the force and rhythm of Barnett's charismatic energy.

"I never get bored with his delivery," a fan remarked. "But he's the only one who can do it and get away with it. If anyone else tried his routines, they wouldn't live through it!" Richard Bauman explains: "Storytelling involves a display of competence in the manner of telling the story, which is subject to evaluation for the way it is done. The audience derives enjoyment from the performance in proportion to the skill of the narrator" (1977: 13).

Barnett Imitates a Japanese Tourist

Barnett focused on the broad cultural expressions of his subjects to exaggerate them into humorous routines. Barnett's humor was based on an inversion of the basic ("serious") uses of language and behavior in daily life. Yet it never entirely reflected the "actuals" of whatever ethnic group he was abusing at the moment. Instead, the material was based on the dominant (white, male, middle-class) culture's ethnocentric image of that group. His jokes were concerned with delineating boundaries: binary oppositions between "us" in the square and "them" outside the square, "us" in New York and "them" in New Jersey, "us" the residents of the United States and "them" the foreign tourists. His humor was therefore both familiar and slightly uncomfortable. As anthropologist Edmund Leach observes: "Local custom is quite often organized not simply on the basis that 'we, the X people, do things differently from the Y people,' but on the principle 'our X customs are correct; those lousy Y people just across the valley are obvious barbarians, they do everything back to front!'" (1976: 63).

Barnett also had a unique pitch: of all the square's performers, he alone had the combination of brass, insolence, and self-assurance to collect his money in the *middle* of his show. He would stop in mid-routine and ask: "How many people like my show so far?" Most would respond with applause. That's good," he would say, "'cause I'm going to collect *now*. You all always *leave* later on." He would move around the circle with a paper bag, hurling insults to prompt greater contributions: Here's a quarter, man. Go call your Mama. You obviously ain't supposed to be out."

Though this segment often lasted ten minutes or more, everyone remained in the fountain, watching each other put money in the bag ("Don't put that change in there, it's too heavy! *Paper* money," he would yell) and waiting for the show to continue. Barnett sometimes repeated the routine at the end of the show, collecting twice from the same people, but his fame and theatrical bravado enabled him to accomplish this street performance "miracle"—he never used the usual timing or lines that most performers found necessary to collect funds. Barnett performed, demanded money, and spectators complied. Vera said Barnett averaged about $300 per show.

Howard Smith, of the *Village Voice*, recalls seeing Barnett perform in Sheridan Square, standing on top of a garbage can:

> His routine was rough, he made mistakes in timing, his segues from one anecdote to another lacked flow, but most of the crowd stayed with him. . . . Since then I've watched him often—in Washington Square Park, Sheridan Square, Bryant Park, Bleecker Street—he's played all the choice spots. He kept getting sharper, his material improved, and he learned the subtleties of the street, like how to work to a climax and then go on before large parts of his audience drifted away thinking the performance was over. (1981: 15)

Recalling his earlier performances, Barnett told me that when he first moved to New York from Boston he started noticing street performers. "I saw Tony [Vera] and Philippe [Petit]. So I tried telling some old jokes, and I made $5. That was a lot of money to me." He began to develop material for a street show by working with a tape recorder and in 1978 started working near Petit's spot at Sheridan Square. "My biggest problem was how to get an audience," Barnett recalled. "I'd wait 'til [Petit's] act was finished and then start hollering 'Show Time!' from across the street." In Washington Square, he used

Vera's shows as the cue. By 1981, Barnett's performances were a prime attraction in the square. Declared Howard Smith: "It is clear to me that Charlie is about to happen" (1981: 15).

In April 1983, true to Smith's prediction, Barnett was "discovered." Gregg Mullins of the William Morris Agency offered Barnett a $1.2 million three-picture contract. The contract stipulated, however, that Barnett could no longer perform outdoors. Instead, a performance at Caroline's, a New York nightclub, was arranged. *Variety* reviewed his August 1983 indoor performance:

> He has picked up a lot of comedic talent working Washington Square in Greenwich Village and the streets, even if he didn't acquire manners. He has no organized act, but knows how to work a crowd and make them like him—four letters and all. He gets laughs not wholly on the basis of gags, but on situations that apparently are real. He addresses individuals, not always in a complimentary manner. . . . The streets may have given him shelter, security, and furthered a sense of comedy, but it [sic] has also given him habits that have to be overcome should he ever get ambitions on another level. Otherwise . . . he can go back to giving street shows. (1983a: 84)

In a November 1983 interview published in *People* magazine, Barnett declared he was a combination of Lenny Bruce, Richard Pryor, and Robin Williams.

The following spring, Barnett appeared in Universal Pictures' *D.C. Cab* with "Mr. T." His character, Tyrone Bywater, relied on facial expressions and gestures identical to those he had used in his street show, but they lacked the street's motivating dynamic. An Asian couple's unexplained appearance on the screen, for example, prompted a closeup of Barnett imitating their faces and speaking fake Japanese. Many of Barnett's street lines were integrated into his film performance. "If I want any shit from you, I'll squeeze your head"—a frequent riposte during his outdoor shows—suddenly surfaced during a coffee shop conversation. Barnett seemed to be reading his lines off cue cards—his face rigid, his eyes fixed somewhere below the camera.

New York audiences nevertheless broke into cheers during the film's opening credits. In the Times Square theater in which I saw the premiere, the crowd chanted the familiar: "Charlie . . . Charlie . . .

Charlie" when Barnett first appeared on the screen. In an article entitled "Street Performers Emboldened by Success of Fellow Busker," *Variety* magazine's Joe Cohen (1983) said that the number of New York City street performers increased significantly following Barnett's film debut in *D.C. Cab*. An earlier *Variety* article suggested that Washington Square Park "may become the Manhatttan version of Hollywood's Schwab's Drug Store" (1983: 66).

In March 1985, Barnett was a "special guest star" on NBC's "Miami Vice" series. Once again, he played a jive, street-smart man with a rubber face and razor tongue. He appeared in five brief segments of the one-hour show. In the first segment, he wore pilot's goggles and a rainbow-colored scarf and rode a surgical gurney around in a bar.

Later that year, it was rumored that Barnett had developed a drug habit and that his contract might be canceled. "Maybe he'll come back to the square," Vera said hopefully. Charlie Barnett was greatly missed in Washington Square, not only by Vera but also by most of the square's regular visitors and performers. Said Vera: "He was my other half. It's just not the same now that he's gone."

FIVE

The King of Washington Square Park

Well-used open spaces in the city often have a "mayor," observes William H. Whyte: "He may be a building guard, a newsstand operator, or a food vendor. Watch him, and you'll notice people checking in during the day—a cop, bus dispatcher, various street professionals, and office workers and shoppers who pause briefly for a salutation or a bit of banter. Plaza mayors are great communication centers, and very quick to spot any departure from normal" (1980: 64). Tony Vera called himself the king of Washington Square; Whyte would no doubt have called him the mayor. Throughout the weekend, regular visitors stopped to pass the time with Vera as "communication center," sharing news and gossip, cigarettes and beer. "Who's working today?" "Heard from Charlie?" "When's your show?" "Did you hear Jim got busted doing his show over on Sixth Ave?"

Vera performed within the traffic flow from Washington Arch and the volatile movement of the circle, in a position just south of the arch. His terrain was the square's prime street performance location, and he remained there throughout the day, either performing or speaking with fans and visitors during breaks. Concerning his location, Vera said:

Tony Vera, The King of Washington Square Park

"No one bothers it at all. Nobody bugs me. The cops know this is my turf. Anyone works it, the cops move 'em. It's like respect." He performed nearly every Saturday and Sunday, usually arriving around noon, and presented five to ten shows daily, each twenty to thirty minutes in duration. Each show attracted an average of two to three hundred spectators.

Vera's act was best known for the lighter fluid he spit out of his mouth and ignited into five- to ten-foot fireballs, but this was only a portion of his act. In a well-rehearsed routine repeated with little variation throughout the day, Vera mixed comedy, magic, and juggling with his dramatic fireblowing tricks. He balanced not only a bicycle but also a small boy perched on a folding chair on his chin. He supervised an eating contest between three young volunteers. A man stood patiently in the center of the performance space while Vera surrounded him with a ring of lighter fluid that he ignited to Indian war whoops and cheers from the audience. Another volunteer jogged around the inner boundary of the Performance Ring while Vera chased him with a fire torch.

Vera began his show by drawing a chalk circle on the sidewalk south of the arch and writing his name around its perimeter. Within minutes, people would gather around in anticipation. Vera, however, paid no attention to the audience, instead focusing on placing his props—a fire extinguisher, a folding chair, six cans of lighter fluid, body-building equipment, Chinese linking rings, ropes, torches, a pitcher of lighter fluid—in a specific and invariant arrangement along the eastern portion of his circle. These props served both as basic scenery and as devices to attract the curious.

Vera walked around his circle, slowly inspecting the area for debris and using a small whisk broom to clean it. He then circled the area more rapidly with an expression of deep concentration. Often it seemed as if he were weaving the spell of his "magic circle." During the last of these circuits, he increased his speed while blowing a whistle around his neck and adjusting the crowd along the inner boundary of his chalk circle, signaling for others to move up.

Throughout his show, Vera communicated entirely with gestures, facial expressions, and a series of rhythmic tones produced by his whistle. Vera said he first chose to use the whistle because he was self-conscious about his Puerto Rican accent. Later, he said, he discovered he could speak "any language of the world" with his whistles and gestures. In fact, nearly every one of Vera's complicated routines was clear to his volunteers and his audience. Occasionally, someone in the audience would become his "translator," shouting: "He wants a cigarette!" "Give him your jacket!" Most gestures, however, were easily understood.

Vera performed in the square throughout my documentation period. His show was so much a part of the square and was performed so consistently in the space that it invites a variety of interpretive approaches concerning its meaning in the urban environment. First, however, it is important to envision the entire act. The fundamental structure of Vera's performance text, from week to week and year to year, is outlined below.

THE SHOW BEGINS

As an initial, audience-gathering device, Vera presented a *handkerchief trick*, pushing a handkerchief into his left fist, standing for a moment, then dramatically removing it from the *same* fist. Though it is clearly not a trick, he moves grandly into the center of the circle, raising his arms and demanding applause. The audience usually responds and

Vera's First Trick

Vera in turn supplies a noble bow. From the moment he first acknowledges them, Vera begins to train his audience in the appropriate codes of exchange for his show.

Vera then pulls a young child into the circle. He pushes the handkerchief into his left fist and indicates that the child is to point to the fist hiding the handkerchief. Since the child saw Vera place the handkerchief, it is easy to choose. The child indicates the left fist and Vera pulls out the handkerchief. Vera then reaches into his pocket and produces a dollar bill, indicating, through mime and whistle, that he will give this dollar to the child if she or he can guess correctly the second time. The child does (because Vera makes no effort to hide the handkerchief), and Vera hands over the dollar.

Vera repeats the trick several more times, still making little or no effort to conceal the handkerchief, grabbing dollars out of his bag and shoving them toward the child. Soon, the child holds a fistful of dollar bills and the audience is laughing in amazement. What street performer gives money away? The display of money, especially money being given away, attracts more people. The crowd is growing.

Finally, Vera blows his whistle and indicates that he will perform the trick one more time. He shoves the handkerchief deeply into one of his fists and holds out his hands for the child to choose. The child points to a fist, and the handkerchief is not there. The child may point to the other fist, but it is not there either. Vera yanks the money away and pulls the handkerchief from his mouth. The audience laughs and applauds. Vera shakes his young volunteer's hand and gives the youngster a dollar, demonstrating a compassion that will later improve his donations. Most important, a central code of exchange—the dollar bill—has been introduced. He gestures for applause as he helps the child to bow.

Vera begins the *cigarette bit* by moving toward someone who is smoking, indicating he wants a cigarette. The spectator pulls out a cigarette pack and offers it to Vera. Vera removes a cigarette, hands it to the unsuspecting volunteer, and walks off with the pack. The audience laughs. Vera returns to reverse the arrangement and take the single cigarette.

He moves around the boundary of his circle, flicking his thumb and forefinger. Someone produces a match; Vera lights the cigarette and steps into the center of his circle. He lays the lit cigarette on his tongue and seems to swallow it. He sticks his tongue out and it is gone. Looking distressed, he begins to exhale great quantities of smoke. He moves around the circle, indicating that he needs something to drink. Someone offers him a soda, he drinks, and exhales more smoke. The audience applauds. Vera returns to the center and "coughs up" the cigarette. He bows and the audience applauds again.

Balancing tricks begin when Vera borrows a bicycle from someone in the crowd, moving through the audience to the owner and exchanging the fireman's hat he wears for the bicycle. Vera than borrows a paper bag from another spectator, tearing off a portion of the bag and placing it in his mouth (this will protect his teeth and lips in the balancing routine he is about to demonstrate). He lifts the bicycle and balances it on the wadded-up paper on his lower lip. The crowd gasps and applauds.

This routine, however, is only a setup for the one to come. Returning the bicycle and retrieving his hat, Vera chooses a youngster from the crowd. He places the volunteer on a folding chair in the center of his circle. Following a brief set of whispered instructions, Vera raises both child and chair to his chin, balancing them high over the heads of his spectators and moving around the circle for five to ten seconds. The crowd is, of course, tremendously impressed and responds with even greater enthusiasm.

The *eating contest* starts when enough children are present. Vera selects three youngsters, usually no more than seven or eight years old, and brings them into the center. Arranging them in a line facing south, he dashes out of the circle to a nearby vendor, making a passageway in the crowd. He returns with either ice cream sandwiches or hot dogs, bringing the items back one at a time while blowing his whistle.

Vera then indicates through mime that his volunteers are about to engage in an eating contest. The first to finish his or her food will receive a dollar bill. He repeats his mimed instructions until he is certain the contestants as well as the audience understand the rules. He then blows his whistle for the contest to begin.

Vera runs back and forth in front of the youngsters, hurrying them along, taunting them with the dollar bill. If a child is having particular difficulty, Vera may run by and take a large bite for him or her. The

Vera Balancing A Boy on a Folding Chair

excited audience yells encouragement, pointing and laughing at the struggling contestants. Finally, Vera declares a winner and awards yet another dollar bill. The audience applauds as the children bow and are returned to the crowd.

A variation in this routine involves two older boys, ten to twelve years of age, in a drinking contest. The format is the same, but canned soda is used instead of food. Vera also watches the boys more carefully: as soon as a small amount of soda inevitably dribbles down a contestant's chin, Vera halts the action. In a routine he will repeat several times, Vera walks to the other boy and pours a small amount of his soda onto the sidewalk, to make things "equal." The action then resumes.

Each contest is conducted in earnest by Vera—he mirrors the seriousness and concentration of his contestants. His sense of fair play, childlike exaggeration, and attention to detail further amuse the audience.

The *sport coat trick* follows the eating contest. Vera circles the inner boundary until he spots a man wearing a sport coat. He pulls the man into the circle and asks the audience to applaud. By now they are well coached and quickly do so. He removes the man's sport coat and pushes him back outside the circle. He looks at the label and laughs silently, looking at the man.

Vera repeats the gesture used earlier to acquire a cigarette. Occasionally, he pulls a lit cigarette from someone's mouth. He moves a few feet, returns, and offers the smoker a puff on the stolen cigarette. The person complies. Vera turns away, then turns back and offers another puff. Again the person complies, Vera turns away, then turns back. Vera repeats the routine until the smoker refuses the proffered cigarette, laughing.

Vera returns to the center, the sport coat in one hand, the cigarette in the other. He takes the coat and makes a small pocket in it. He then pushes the lit cigarette into the indentation, shifts his weight on one hip, freezes, and stares at the coat's owner. The audience laughs. Depending on their response, he may acquire another cigarette to repeat the routine. He will also smoke the cigarette periodically to show that it is still lit inside the coat.

Finally, he mashes the cigarette out while it is (or at least appears to be) inside the coat pocket. He inspects the lining. Slowly, he looks at the owner and mouths silently with great exaggeration: "I'M SORRY." Following a brief but tension-filled pause, he shakes the coat open and circles the audience to show that it is unharmed. Vera bows and the audience applauds.

To begin the *kissing bit,* Vera strolls around the circle, looking at the audience. He moves to a young woman and takes her newspaper, sunglasses, sweater, and so on, carelessly handing the items to people around her. She is pulled into the center, often protesting loudly. Sometimes, Vera will simply make the audience applaud and then push her back to the circle, selecting another woman instead. (Vera says he judges his participants carefully, looking for particular personalities for each routine. If he thinks he has misjudged, he will simply return his volunteer to the circle following the applause—the audience thinks it's funny.)

Once Vera has selected his female volunteer, he chooses a male volunteer. In the gesture he has established in both the handkerchief trick and the eating contest, Vera pulls a dollar out of his pocket, snaps it, and shows it to the crowd. Then he points to the man's pocket and repeats the snapping gesture. The man produces a dollar bill. Vera has the man hold the bill over his head. Vera turns to the woman. He makes a kissing noise and points to the man's cheek. Often, the woman refuses to kiss the man. "Go on, kiss him," someone in the audience may yell. Eventually, with sufficient coaxing, she kisses the man and the audience applauds. Immediately, Vera yanks the dollar out of the man's hand and gives it to the woman, pushing the man out of the circle. He then tips the woman backward, kisses her, and yanks the bill out of her hand, pushing her out of the circle as well. Following the crowd's laughter and applause, Vera will return the dollar to the man.

Between each of the performance segments described above, Vera may employ several additional bits of business. He may, for example, see a bald man standing on the inner boundary of his space and kiss him on the top of his head several times during the show. He may see someone with a dog and move toward the dog with his hand outstretched and pet the owner instead. Several of Vera's more flexible routines depend upon available props or volunteers.

Additionally, regular fans sometimes bring their own tricks. Once a couple brought champagne for Vera to drink during the cigarette-swallowing segment. A boy brought some matches that reignited each time Vera shook or blew them out. Others stood in front with cigarettes, beer, cameras, paper bags, and the other items Vera requests during the show.

At last, Vera begins the *fire torches* segment, picking up the torches that have been soaking in lighter fluid throughout the show. He moves around the circle, using the now familiar thumb-flicking gesture to obtain a match. He lights the torches. Tourists usually grab their cameras at this point, and Vera will stop, hamming it up for several moments—lying down on the sidewalk, posing like a Hollywood starlet, pulling up his shirt, and so on.

He balances one of the torches on his nose, moving around the circle. He demands applause. Not satisfied, he demands louder ap-

Vera and Fire Torch

Vera Swallows Fire

plause, looking irritated. When he gets the applause he wishes, he bows grandly. Vera kneels and puts the torch into his mouth several times, exhaling small breaths of fire each time he removes it.

The audience is ready for the finale, Vera's legendary fireblowing routine. But Vera suddenly stops and pulls another man out of the circle, usually someone middle-aged and overweight. He grabs a bodybuilding gadget, a device featuring several coiled springs between two handles. He pulls the handles apart with a groan. "Now you try it," he seems to say to the man, patting him on the arm. The man can barely pull the handles apart. Vera repeats the routine several times, finally wagging his wrist at the man in a stereotypical gesture of effiminacy.

Returning to his torches, Vera signals the man to remain in the circle. He indicates that his victim can rescue his masculinity by waving his hand over a torch. The man does so. Vera then holds his palm out for the man to slap in a recognizable gesture of greeting among African-American males. The man slaps Vera's palm. Vera returns the gesture and offers his hand again. The man slaps his palm, Vera returns the slap. They repeat the ritual several times with increasing speed. Finally, as the man begins to slap Vera's palm, Vera quickly substitutes the flaming torch he has been holding in his other hand. The man stops in alarm and everyone laughs.

Next, Vera moves his volunteer into a small chalk circle drawn within the larger chalk boundary of his performance space. While the man stands patiently, Vera pours lighter fluid into his mouth and spits it over the torch, igniting a flaming stream of liquid. Vera repeats the trick, staring intently at the man with a mock threatening expression. Vera looks very serious, however, as he tosses the man a fire extinguisher. He picks up a can of lighter fluid. Blowing on his whistle, Vera runs around the man, squirting a circle of fluid onto the sidewalk. He saturates the ground in a three-inch band around his unsuspecting participant and lights it. The flames are low but spread quickly, and Vera reaches over to grab the man's fire extinguisher. It does not work, and Vera flings it to the ground, where it breaks into several pieces. As the flames quickly subside, Vera asks the audience to applaud the volunteer.

If the fire-sequence volunteer is especially trusting, Vera may insert

Vera Blows Fire

an additional segment: he will place an unlit cigarette in the man's mouth, fill his own mouth with lighter fluid and, holding the torch between his mouth and the man's cigarette, begin to aim at the man's cigarette. He will adjust his position several times, approach the man and tear off part of the cigarette to make the trick more difficult, and generally prepare, stop, and delay for a prolonged period. By the time Vera has finished, the cigarette will be just a stub and the man will be standing very, very still. Vera will then look at the man with a pitying expression. He will pretend to swallow the fluid (which he actually never had in his mouth), and then lead the man to the small inner circle to begin the fluid-encircling routine. This entire volunteer sequence is part of a range of street (and circus) techniques known as the "drag out." The performer indicates an intended routine—in Vera's case, the fireblowing finale—but then drags out the time until its actual enactment to increase an audience's interest and enthusiasm.

At last, however, Vera will conclude the show with several very grand eight- to ten-foot fireballs, created by spitting lighter fluid out of his mouth and igniting it. He is concentrated and precise during this

Passing the Hat

sequence, demonstrating skill, confidence, and control, though he often uses another drag out—repeatedly checking wind direction, for example—to heighten the audience's anticipation. The fireballs are nevertheless a very impressive trick, and spectators always feel this segment was well worth the wait. Many remark that they felt the heat from the fire some distance away—"Wow, it was *really hot!*"

Immediately following the climactic fireblowing, Vera bows a final time with the serious expression he has used several times during the show to gain maximum recognition. He quickly indicates, however, that the audience should acknowledge him in some other way: clapping his hands in imitation, he looks at the audience and shakes his head. He removes his hat and displays the now familiar dollar bill gesture he has established as a code of exchange. He throws the imaginary bill into his hat. As he moves around the circle, nearly everyone waits to place a dollar in his hat. Often, five and even ten dollar bills are evident. The audience has read the codes of Vera's presentation and learned to respond enthusiastically to each of his requests. It was also a very good show.

THE STREET AS STAGE

Street performance, like its close cousin, environmental theater, places greatest emphasis on "physicalization rather than verbalization" (Jerry Rojo, in McNamara, Rojo, and Schechner, 1975: 14). Vera mimed and gestured throughout his performance. He balanced both a bicycle and a child perched on a folding chair. He blew fire and performed magic. Yet there was no dialogue, no patter. Vera's act focused exclusively, and very successfully, on behavior and interaction.

Certainly simplicity was a large part of his show's attractiveness—it required little effort to watch or participate in his routines. Most street shows use familiar jokes or tricks with predictable outcomes (Vera's handkerchief trick; Chang's clichéd jokes; the inevitable slow transit of Cohen's racing turtles). Yet the performance moves within an audience's "horizon of expectations" (H. R. Jauss, in Pavis, 1982: 74), and the spectator is familiar with similar performance texts, which actually enable appropriate decoding. Additionally, a certain flexibility must be built into the street act to allow for the unpredictability of both the environment and the audience. Helicopters, barking dogs, traffic, babies, hecklers—all become the stuff of outdoor performance, and the better a performer can transform these potential disruptions into entertaining diversions and witty commentaries on urban life, the more successful he will be.

Storyteller Carl Asche mentioned his admiration for Vera's ability to use a variety of external intrusions during his show:

> One thing Tony did that I thought was one of the greatest things I'd ever seen was when he lit one of his fire torches and a fire alarm went off somewhere. He looked up, looked around in confusion and panic, gave the torch to somebody in the audience, and left! Just stood in the audience, going "La dee da, I don't know what's going on." And it appeared to the audience that it was phenomenally spontaneous. I'm sure that it had happened before but, you know, it was just perfectly timed. It's a very flowing thing.

I mentioned the fire torch routine to Vera. He said he listened for the alarm to go off during his act, and if the coincidence occurred, he used it. He could not plan on it, but he hoped for it, thus structuring his text to allow for the intrusion of the environment.

Commedia Dell'Arte, an Italian performance form popular from the sixteenth to the nineteenth centuries, offers a useful historical parallel, for Vera's use of coincidence has its counterpart in the Commedia actor's use of "lazzi." The lazzi was a routine or series of routines introduced at will during individual performances. Each was pulled from a stock of dependable gags—bits of physical or verbal business that had proven successful in previous performances. Favorite routines included mime, such as trying to catch an imaginary fly buzzing around one's head, slapstick encounters with objects (ladders were popular), or set verbal exchanges between actors.

Contemporary street performers use lazzi throughout their improvised outdoor shows. Cohen called them "canned ripostes." Vera included bald men, dogs, children, and bicycles, as well as Asche's favorite siren routine. Barnett would wait for hecklers to interrupt him and then announce: "Give to the United Negro College Fund, folks. As you can see, a mind is a terrible thing to waste!" And though each performer repeated his stock remarks in many performances, the lazzi always seemed freshly invented for the situation at hand.

True spontaneity, however, is rare. Most performers move between the fixed and the flexible, constructing a street text based on the most predictable audience or environmental cues. Explained Asche: "My show is planned out—every gesture is sculpted into it—but for an audience it's a very spontaneous thing." Performers recognize the importance of engaging their audience as directly as possible but also know that they must maintain control of the event. Here, too, street performance shares with environmental theater an ability to create audience participation "precisely at that point where the performance breaks down and becomes a social event" (Schechner, 1973: 40), but only within a core that is planned out in advance.

Most street shows follow a set outline of events. A performer will generally begin his show with a series of slow warm-up routines to gather an audience. He then moves into a wider range of medium-paced tricks or dialogue to maintain a crowd. These routines will ultimately lead to a climactic finale that ends abruptly—the performer's objective in this final phase is to convert the audience's enthusiasm into maximum contributions.

Often, the timing of the entire street performance is built around the crucial final phase—the pitch. The rhythm and style of the overall show, in fact, are reminiscent of the "jo-ha-kyu" (slow-medium-fast) rhythm of Japanese *Noh* performances. I once asked Petit to describe the way he ended his street act. He answered with one word: "fast." A moment's hesitation, as Peter Shub learned, or the stubborn inclusion of a humorous denouement, as in Cohen's award ceremony, may leave the performer with an empty hat. Street performers learn that the pitch must be precisely timed to transform and audience's greatest emotional energy into the greatest number of dollar bills.

Drag outs were a popular street device for increasing the audience's response to an act. Vera prolonged the time between preparing for and actually performing his climactic fireblowing segment; Carol Mills extended her unicycle performance by feigning fear, inexperience, or difficulty mounting the bike; Barnett interrupted his show to pass the hat. Cohen introduced "Y. A. Turtle" before starting the race. Each performer would indicate that a potentially humorous or dazzling routine was about to begin and then drag out the time until its actual enactment.

Drag outs are common in circus performances as well and usually for the same reasons: the trick actually requires preparation and/or quiet and concentration; or the performer simply wants to maximize the audience's concentration, emotional involvement, and response to the intended routine. Vera's concluding fireballs fit both categories, but the second—in which Vera would needlessly check and recheck the wind's speed and direction, for example—was primarily a device designed to increase contributions.

Figure 22 illustrates a typical street performance text. The show is ordinarily accomplished within twenty minutes, a time frame enabling an audience to grasp the act as a whole. Letters A, B, and C represent three basic segments or routines in the show. The lines between segments represent several potential paths to these routines; the smaller circles represent some of the random tricks that may be selected during individual performances.

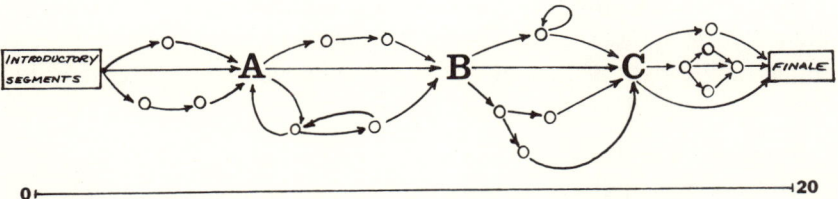

FIGURE 22: The Street Performance Text

The lines and small circles are the most flexible and spontaneous parts of a street show and include all the lazzi proven successful in previous performances. Each may be lengthened or shortened depending on audience response. Routes within each performance of the text may overlap, double back, even repeat. Certain favorite or reliably entertaining tricks will appear in each performance, the duration of each controlled by the audience. In a variety of ways, Vera's and other Washington Square performances carry an "emergent quality" that "resides in the interplay between communicative resources, individual competence, and the goals of the participants, within the context of particular situations" (Bauman, 1977: 38).

I asked Vera to describe his street performance text and its development. He answered: "You work every day in the streets and find out what you're doing wrong, okay? And you're doing something wrong, you don't do that. Try something else. It works, keep it in the act. Keep doing it 'til your act is polished." What did he mean when he said something "works"? He replied: "People laugh, they have a good time, and mostly you can tell by what's in your hat at the end of the show. If it didn't work, that means not as much money—and vice versa."

Essentially, then, the street performer constructs his performance text through a process of trial and error, adding, removing, or revising segments of his individual routines in a process of constant, often moment-to-moment revision. Each adjustment is prompted by ideas about what "works" in the show, that is, what entertains an audience and results in the greatest profits. But Vera is not selecting parts at random; rather, he is dealing with the performance text as a whole, in which each choice affects the subsequent choices of his act.

Vera's opening strategy—the concentrated placement of props while ignoring the audience—is especially interesting, for it reflects a technique dating back at least as far as medicine show performers. In his book *Step Right Up*, McNamara reports:

> Professor Ray Black developed an impressive scheme for drawing a crowd that centered around a length of rope, a Bible, and a human skull. In a town square or a vacant lot on a busy street, Black would lay out his strange properties, placing them on the ground next to his folding table and medicine case. Then he would arrange and rearrange them. Apparently oblivious to the fascinated crowd that gradually gathered around him, Black would continue his curious work for half an hour or more until he was satisifed with the size of his tip [audience]. Then he would suddenly begin his medicine lecture, never once mentioning in it the Bible, rope or skull. (1976: 24)

Central Park magician Jeff Sheridan, who claims Vera learned many of his tricks by watching Sheridan's 1976–78 performances, describes a similar opening in a 1976 interview with Susan Condos:

> Purposefully, I'll be oblivious to everything around me—noise, traffic, people, everything. I ignore the audience and just get involved with doing magic. I'm performing to the tree that's facing me. I think the fact that I'm oblivious to the audience attracts them. Their curiosity is aroused by my self absorption, and they want to know more about that. At one point, I'll look up and find an audience there. (1976: 56)

Yet as mentioned earlier, chains of transmission are difficult to trace in street shows. It is difficult to tell who is borrowing from whom—street performance is part of the public domain, in all that this phrase implies.

Starting the show was sometimes a problem for other performers in the square. Barnett, Chang, and the Millses began their shows by getting a few people to applaud and scream, drawing attention and thus more people to the area. Everyone was curious about who was having fun. They also maximized their initial audiences by starting their shows just as Vera's audience dispersed. Chang also described a supplemental audience-gathering technique he called "doubling." He would begin with a magic trick for one person. That person would attract another. Those two became four, four became eight, and so on. He said he would begin juggling when a "critical mass" was achieved.

I asked Cohen how he decided to begin his shows. I had noticed that he seemed to study the crowd, looking for something particular as he walked around his set. He answered:

> I study geometry, I study body language, and I know from the beginning whether it's a good audience or whether I should wait a while longer and let these people flake off so I can collect some new ones who'll stay.
>
> I don't like dull-faced people. I don't like vacuous looking people. I like people who have some alertness in their faces, people who I know somehow will appreciate it.
>
> I hate audiences that form in knots, leaving gaps all around the track. I like to look out at a sea of faces in which I know everyone is concentrating.
>
> I don't like hippy-dippy kids on roller skates who'll wind up performing just as much as I am.
>
> Definitely I case the crowd. A lot of times, if I'm not happy with the crowd, you'll notice that I'll say, "the next race will be in five minutes." That's a test. If they're interested enough to hang around for five minutes, they'll be an okay crowd.

Each performer, then, had particular strategies for timing the opening of the show, maintaining a crowd, and soliciting contributions. Choices were based on the unique combination of each show and its setting.

FOLK HEROES OF THE URBAN ENVIRONMENT

Paul Bouissac identifies five progressive stages in a typical circus act. He associates these with messages of survival and goes on to assess a variety of circus acts in semiotic terms. The five stages he constructs also mirror the structure of street performances:

1. Identification of the hero, who incidentally is often introduced as a non-autochthon [non-native].
2. Qualifying test, which the artist considers as a warm-up exercise.
3. Main test, which can consist of several tests presented in a variety of sequences.

4. Glorifying test, which is usually preceded by a special announcement and accompanied by a drum roll.

5. Public acknowledgment of the fulfillment of the task. (Bouissac, 1976: 25)

Chang, Barnett, and Vera all introduced themselves as "outsiders" or non-natives (Chang in particular played up his Asian appearance). Vera presented himself as a non-native by indicating that he would communicate nonverbally, through mime and whistles. Vera then presented a qualifying test (the handkerchief trick), several main tests (balancing, eating contests, kissing, preliminary torch routines), and a final glorifying test (the climactic fireblowing). Public acknowledgment occurred when he passed the hat.

The clarity of these five stages is important, Bouissac says, because "anyone who is accustomed to circus shows can arrive while an act is in progress and be able to say with significant accuracy whether the act is just starting, is in the middle, or is near the end" (1976: 24). This is true of much street performance as well. I often saw visitors arrive for Vera's show who clearly knew exactly where he was in the performance. I was also able to identify these stages in new acts I encountered in midshow.

Bouissac further divides jugglers' and magicians' acts into three phases: "construction of a situation, introduction of a disrupting factor, and control of the disruption." These, he notes, may be further divided into subsequences that are set apart by short pauses. Each sequence is performed in order of "increasing drama, i.e., increasing degree of disturbance that must be controlled to ensure the survival of the artist" (1976: 70).

The individual segments of Vera's show also occurred in these three phases. Vera first *constructed the situation*, selecting audience members who would participate, presenting the rules of the particular game, collecting the necessary props, or indicating an intended action. He then *introduced a disrupting factor*, usually simply by relying on certain characteristic responses to the proposed text, or sometimes by presenting an impossibility (putting fire in one's mouth, using a fire extinguisher that does not work). Finally, he *controlled the disruption*, convincing his participant to play by the rules, making the eating or drinking contest more "equal," and saving his victim from the situation he had created.

This sequence has significant parallels in classic literary tales of heroism as well. In folktales, for example, the hero typically encounters a situation that must be resolved. One or more disrupting factors are introduced—riddles, trolls, rivers—which the hero ultimately overcomes. In street performance, however, the audience participates in the heroic event by creating, judging, or actively assisting in the hero's tests. Heroic representatives from the audience are tested—made to kiss one another, tug on exercise equipment, and so on. The empathetic relationship between audience and performer is therefore enhanced, promoting a feeling of collective heroism. Then, in Vera's climactic fireblowing sequence, he elaborately fills his mouth with lighter fluid, swishing it around in his mouth, walking around the circle, displaying his torches; introduces a disrupting factor by focusing on the wind's direction and where he shall spit the flame, occasionally responding to sirens or helicopters; and successfully ignites the fluid. At this moment, the emotional response of his audience reaches it highest point in the show. The crowd cheers with tremendous enthusiasm. The conversion occurs: removing his hat, Vera indicates that a different affirmation of their approval, enjoyment, and understanding of his show is now necessary. The audience inevitably responds to Vera's heroic mastery, and Vera has by now established the dollar bill as the acceptable form of tribute.

THE MAGIC CIRCLE

"Circus," Bouissac said, "is a semiotic crucible in which our cultural reality is systematically and significantly transformed for the length of the performance" (1976: 7). So too for street performance. Vera works within the crucible of Washington Square Park, his performance text reflecting the striving of anonymous city dwellers to achieve a mark of individuality through wit, skills, even silliness. Through humor, he provides opportunities to laugh at our fears. Through balancing feats, he presents a symbolic victory over space and gravity. Through magic and illusion, he gives a sense of control over objects. Like circus, the "meaning" of a street performance text "is based on each act's particu-

Peter Shub with Hand Puppet

lar relevance to those structures that constitute the culture of the country in which the acts are being performed, i.e. the 'contextual culture'" (Bouissac, 1976: 66).

In New York, performing outside working hours, the street performer punctuates the otherwise homogenous reality of everyday life. Through feats of dexterity and skill, he leads an audience into a temporary world of wonders. Vera shows us men fearful of having their clothing burned or their masculinity challenged; he instructs women to kiss strangers for money. Yet "within the Magic Circle, every action grows into balletic motion and accent: the lifting of a child or of a grail, the imitations of beasts and birds, the kiss, the war whoop. Free dance movement produces, above all (for the performer as well as the spectator) the illusion of a conquest of gravity" (Langer, 1953: 194).

The rhythms of Washington Square are transformed every Saturday and Sunday afternoon by the events performed in it. The spectator moves into and explores a number of different events occurring simultaneously, creating opportunities to inject his or her personality into the acts and thus define theatrical space in a more active and creative way. Street performers in Washington Square respond to the complex, competitive demands of a large urban space. Audiences demonstrate their understanding and appreciation of the performer's communicative actions through laughter, applause, and giving money. The final performance text, then, is written between the performer and the audience.

SIX

Drawing a Circle in the Square

The fundamental sociability of the performance experience is revealed in the square's very structure. Curving pathways, circular sitting areas, benches and ledges surrounding a central fountain area—all prompt circular gatherings of spectators and circling patterns of movement through the space. Public reflexivity is built into the square, stimulating performative behavior among all who visit the space. It is not only a theatre in the round, it is a revolving theatre in the round, offering multiple viewing and performance opportunities, choice in consumption, and the possibility of the unexpected. It is an environment that must be "understood as a complex set of relationships between time, space, actions, objects. At each level and during each transaction a negotiation takes place" (Schechner, 1969: 198).

Milling increases the level of general excitement. "It attracts, and infects individuals, many of whom originally are merely detached and indifferent spectators and bystanders. At first, people may be merely curious about the given behavior, or mildly interested in it. As they catch the spirit of excitement and become more attentive to the behavior, they become more inclined to engage in it" (Blumer, 1946: 176).

Spectators may suddenly create new spatial possibilities, spontaneously gathering around a group of breakdancers, a flashy Frisbee player, a wino dancing in the fountain, a fistfight. And the notion that Washington Square's street shows occur outside the system of commercial entertainment heightens the spectators' sense of personal potency—audiences feel they are participating in, even creating, the theatrical events of the square.

Focus in the square is therefore flexible and multiple. Spectators watching a juggler may hear a nearby rock band or see another, perhaps more interesting performance begin across the square. Some will wander away to watch. Others will watch from the juggler's circle—creating a viewing phenomenon Schechner once described as "selective inattention," in which "spectators come and go, pay attention or don't, select what parts of the performance to follow" (1977: 156).

Street performers must pay careful attention to events happening elsewhere. In Washington Square, for instance, up to twenty performers were sometimes working simultaneously on a sunny weekend afternoon, each seeking to attract the largest audience and thereby the greatest contributions of the day. By midafternoon, thousands of people were walking, wandering, and watching, creating their own structure of performance viewing by choosing which presentation to attend next. An accomplished performer must therefore entertain a wide range of people who wander by and will continue to wander on if not effectively held by his act.

Costumes and props help the performer to maintain focus by setting him apart as an entertainer. They are also easily identified in large crowds and command the necessary attention for the show to begin. Certainly showmanship helped the outdoor performer attract a transient audience. But performers had to devise ways not only to attract an audience but also to control the potentially volatile gathering once it was created.

Indoor theaters have a comprehensive system of behavior codes and controlling conventions to circumvent the power of an emotionally wrought-up crowd. Conventional theater also tends toward sociofugality: each spectator has his or her own well-marked space and relative immunity from physical or visual contact with others in the audience. The result is an emphasis on personal rather than social per-

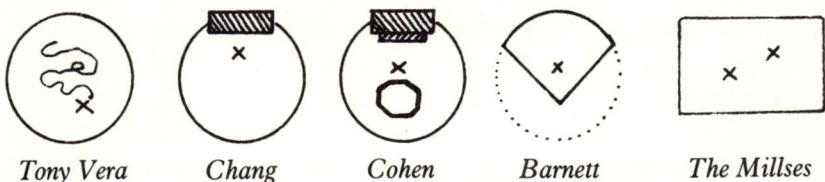

| Tony Vera | Chang | Cohen | Barnett | The Millses |

FIGURE 23: Performance Stages of Washington Square

ceptions and responses. The sociopetality of Washington Square's performances, on the other hand, with audiences clustered in circles around the individual performers, emphasizes the collective origins of performance. Thus street performers must first negate the passivity of indoor audiences so that their audiences' energy and enthusiasm are converted into contributions and then focus and control that energy, for the situation can be dangerous. Even Vera was violently attacked in 1984, when a man wielding a knife leaped into Vera's circle and punctured his lung.

Some street performers simply rely on "safety in numbers," in which the will of the many controls the few—a system Kenneth Burke called an "attitude of collaborative expectancy" (1969: 58). Others establish clear territorial boundaries. Petit, Vera, and the Millses, for instance, defined their territories with chalk, marking a tangible boundary on the previously undefined space of a public sidewalk. The chalk circle, set apart from empty space, confined attention and limited activities, thereby defining the situation as a theatrical one. Charlie Barnett, on the other hand, used the natural boundary of the fountain to delimit his performance space. But each performer developed a specific spatial configuration, based on personal preference, performance requirements, environmental demands, and particular skills (see Figure 23).

Certainly a circle is the most sensible arrangement out-of-doors, for it provides maximum visibility for the greatest number of persons, while assisting in crowd control by placing focus on the center. Spectators may watch each other as well as the show: in several confrontations I witnessed between performers and hecklers, the audience rather than the performer ejected the unruly member by shouting him or her into submission. Circularity promotes shoulder-to-shoulder and across-the-space interaction, a shared focus, a heightening of interest and participation. "If individuals are randomly distributed over a flat surface in the starting situation," note Stanley Milgram and Hans Toch, "a point of common interest in the same plane creates a crowd tending toward circularity. The circular arrangement is not accidental but serves an important function. It permits the most efficient arrangement of individuals around a point of common focus" (1969: 518).

AERIAL FIELDWORK

Each weekend in Washington Square, I observed the regular formation and dissolution of circular rings of spectators as well as the aimless milling of individual visitors. The atmosphere in the Performance Ring seemed charged with significance: as rings contracted and expanded, shifting patterns of movement revealed alternating areas of importance. Performance in the square was a dynamic, shifting, breathing event. I began to map its movements, chart its rhythms and durations. On Sunday, September 20, 1981, Tom Mikotowicz and his friend Joe Mosier took a series of photographs to assist in this research.

Mikotowicz and Mosier took one photograph every minute for slightly over nine and a half hours (10:00 A.M. to 7:37 P.M.) from the roof of New York University's twelve-story Bobst Library on the southeast corner of Washington Square. It was an ideal street performance day, partly sunny and breezy, with temperatures ranging from 59 to 75 degrees. The goal was to document the movements of the crowds and the activities of street performers during the prime performance hours in the square. The photographs also provided data to chart the length of individual performances and the exchanges and negotiations between performers.

The performers' locations are shown in Figure 24, while the bar chart (Figure 25) calculates the beginnings and endings of performances throughout the afternoon's photographs. Three musical acts—the Beatles impersonators (#12), the rock musicians (#13), and a bongo player (#14)—not visible in the photographs were instead graphed "by ear." Vendors are omitted from the chart because their activities were continuous.

Mikotowicz and I found that most events were related to the other

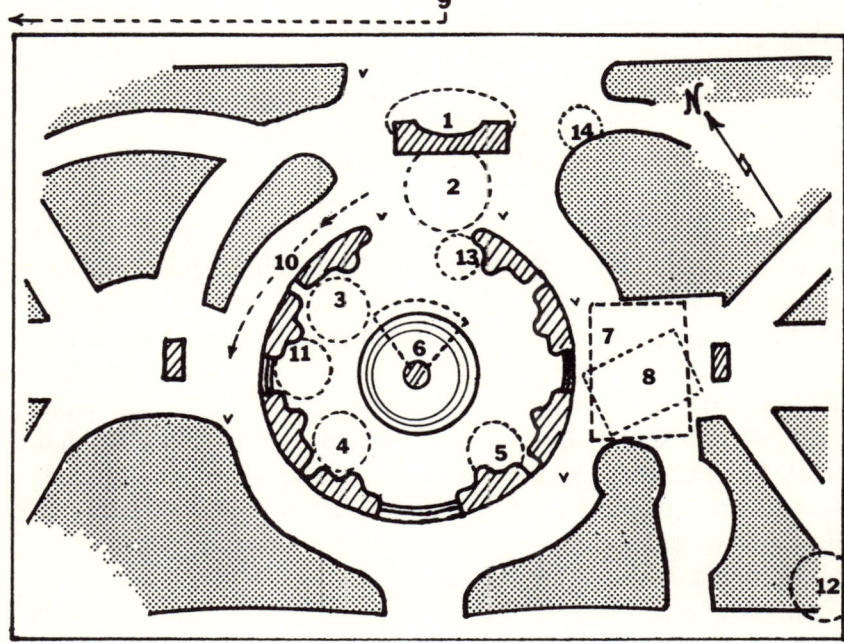

1. Piano player
2. Tony Vera
3. Chang
4. Mime
5. Jazz musicians
6. Charlie Barnett
7. Theatre for the New City
8. Roller skaters
9. Fifth Avenue parade
10. Religious speaker
11. Breakdancers
12. Beatles impersonators
13. Rock musicians
14. Bongo player
v. Vendors

FIGURE 24: Street Performance and Other Activity Locations, September 20, 1981

events. Shows started when others ended; durations fluctuated because of shifting patterns elsewhere in the space. Note, for example, the exchanges between the piano player and Vera in the bar chart (#1 and #2 respectively). Their performance times seem to interchange successively. Figure 24 shows that these performers were only a few feet apart, and interviews confirmed that the alternative structure was based on an agreement between them. Explained Vera: "He plays for

1. Piano player
2. Tony Vera
3. Chang
4. Mime
5. Jazz musicians
6. Charlie Barnett
7. Theatre for the New City
8. Roller skaters
9. Fifth Avenue parade
10. Religious speaker
11. Break dancers
12. Beatles impersonators
13. Rock musicians
14. Bongo player

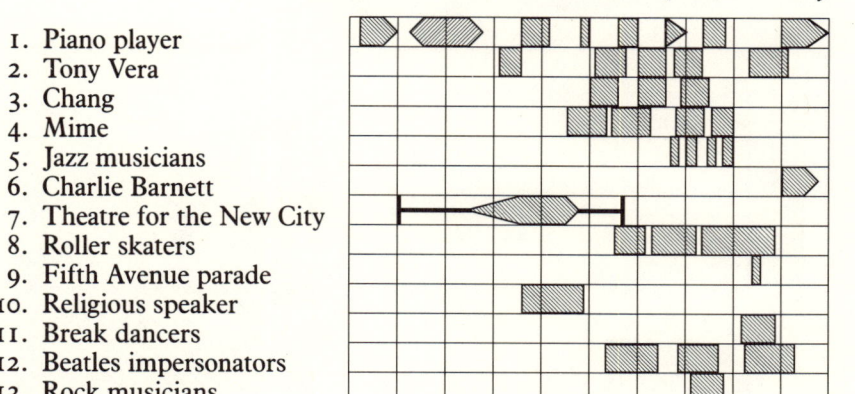

FIGURE 25: Frequencies and Durations of Performances, September 20, 1981

a while, then I perform for a while. We worked it out this summer—we had to. I figure he's my intermission."

Seven months earlier, however, Vera had performed perhaps ten feet south of his September location. His move north also represented his growing confidence as the lead performer (the king) of Washington Square. The "agreement" between Vera and the pianist probably came about only as Vera acquired greater strength in the territory. Clearly his new location challenged the pianist's power in the square. The following year, the piano player did not perform.

It also seems that Chang (#3) and a mime (#4) were more intent on competing than cooperating in the space on September 20. Chang, for example, consistently began his show before the mime could reach the moment of his pitch. One of Chang's three shows also coincided with Vera's show times.

The jazz musicians (#5) had difficulty playing over the amplified sounds of the Beatles impersonators. The chart in Figure 25 therefore shows an irregular series of short musical performances. Mikotowicz said the Beatles group's music overpowered most of the square's other musical events.

Two unusual events further affected the performance patterns on September 20. Theater for the New City, a nearby indoor theater company, held a free performance in the roller skaters' area (#7). Trucks arrived around 11:00 A.M., carrying equipment and a portable stage.

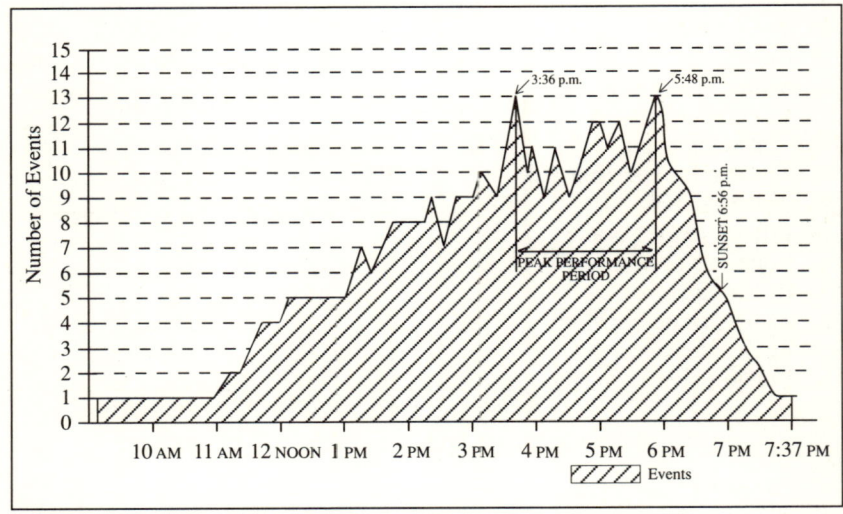

FIGURE 26: Events Over Time = Intensity

Plastic milk cases were set up in rows for seating, and loudspeakers were arranged to face the seats. (Unlike most events in the square, this event was not in-the-round.) Music was broadcast over the loudspeakers between 12:45 P.M. and 1:30 P.M. The performance began at 1:36 P.M., just minutes after Vera's show ended, and lasted one hour.

Neither Vera, Chang, nor the mime performed during the theater event. Chang and Vera began their shows shortly after 3:00 P.M. The group's trucks left by 3:40 P.M. and the roller skaters (#8) regained control of the area for the remainder of the day.

Then, at 6:24 P.M., a parade coming down Fifth Avenue reached the square and turned west along Washington Square North, attracting hundreds of people to the square's northern boundary. Vera began his act at 6:28 P.M. and played to one of the largest audiences of the day. Vera was very good at choosing performance times that coincided with the conclusion of other events, though interviews revealed no conscious decision to do so. Vera simply said he begins his shows "when I'm ready" or "when it feels right."

Mikotowicz and I used the data on all performative behaviors and events (including vendors) to chart the increasing intensity of the square activities (see Figure 26). Mikotowicz recorded event totals at six-minute intervals to determine the average number of performances in progress and compute the peak performance period of the square.

THE PHOTOGRAPHS

It is not feasible to present the entire series of over five hundred aerial photographs, but it may be useful to examine two brief samples, for the photographs display notions of density, accretion, duration, dispersal, and flow that enrich ideas about the total street performance event. The photographs show how space may be defined through the locations and movements of people—how it lies between, around, and among them—and how time is defined in terms of interaction, rhythm, and intensity. From above, the pattern resembles that of iron filings attracted to a series of alternating magnets, as audiences were attracted to and repelled by the different street performers. The reader may also recall that the reason iron filings exhibit patterns is because the field in which they are placed is not homogenous. So too for Washington Square: varying levels of skill among performers, various interests and purposes among spectators, different responses to and uses of the space determine the overall image. Yet an image of community emerges, an "image of 'full roundness' [which] helps us collect ourselves, permits us to confer an initial constitution on ourselves, and confirms our being intimately inside" (Bachelard, 1964: 234).

The series begins with the first photograph of the day: Washington Square Park at 10:00 A.M. Though neither performers nor vendors had arrived, I am reminded of Peter Brook's "empty space": "I can take any empty space and call it a bare stage. A man walks across this empty space whilst someone else is watching him, and that is all that is needed for an act of theatre to be engaged" (1968: 9).

Prime Time. The first sample is from the peak performance time in Washington Square. Usually, prime time was between 2:00 P.M. and 5:00 P.M. On September 20, however, the Theatre for the New City caused the peak street performance hours to shift one hour, to between 3:00 P.M. and 6:00 P.M. The photographs, selected from a series taken between 4:55 P.M. and 5:15P.M., show the dynamics of the square during these hours of greatest performance intensity.

The first photograph, taken at 4:55 P.M., shows Vera's fourth show

The Empty Space: Washington Square, 10:00 a.m.

of the day under way. Additionally, Chang and the mime are starting to attract crowds to their third shows, and the jazz musicians are warming up for their first improvised melody. Within one minute, at 4:56 P.M., the two Performance Ring shows are well established. Note also that the size of Vera's crowd has swelled considerably.

The constellations remain constant through the next eight minutes. By 5:05 P.M., four rings of activity are clearly visible, the jazz musicians having attracted a ring of listeners as well. Barely visible beneath the trees near the arch, a fifth ring partially forms around a rock musician who is beginning to play.

Seven minutes later, at 5:12 P.M., Vera's, Chang's, and the mime's performances remain. The jazz and rock musicians' crowds have dwindled. Music audiences tend to ebb and subside more rapidly than performance audiences.

One minute later, at 5:13 P.M., Vera's audience is dispersing toward the Performance Ring. The rings around Chang and the mime increase, and greater numbers of people are visible in both the ring and

Washington Square, 4:55 p.m.

Washington Square, 4:56 p.m.

Washington Square, 5:05 p.m.

Washington Square, 5:12 p.m.

Washington Square, 5:13 p.m.

Washington Square, 5:14 p.m.

the skaters' areas. By 5:14 P.M., many of Vera's spectators have collected around the piano player, Chang, and the mime. Others are milling about in the ring. Another cycle will begin at 6:28, when Vera begins another show.

Evening. The second series displays the activities of the square as it moves from daylight to nighttime. Said Vera: "Day and night are two different shows here in the square. It's like I'm the sun and Charlie [Barnett]'s the moon. We're day and night, man. And we need each other to keep the place together." The square changes greatly after sunset, and most of the street performances, Barnett's the major exception, occur during the day.

The series begins at sunset, 6:56 P.M. Vera is taking the final bow for his fifth and last performance of the day. Fieldwork suggests that Charlie Barnett is standing nearby, waiting for Vera's show to end. Within one minute, a small group has formed on the northern rim of the fountain, Barnett's performance area, as Vera's crowd thins.

At 6:58 P.M., Barnett's audience builds. Those with either very good eyesight or a magnifying glass may see a dark-skinned man in light clothing strutting before the crowd. Barnett is preparing to use his audience-gathering technique.

6:59 P.M. shows a mild increase in audience size as the audience begins to yell, while 7:01 P.M. and 7:03 P.M. show dramatic leaps in audience size.

The series concludes at 7:12 P.M., as the square's visitors assemble in its center for a final gathering together. Soon, each will return home or move on to other nighttime activities. Yet, as happens every weekend, a special "communitas" was encountered and affirmed in Washington Square. Activities continue in the square well into the night. By early morning hours, the square is once again an empty space.

Washington Square, 6:56 p.m.

Washington Square, 6:57 p.m.

Washington Square, 6:58 p.m.

Washington Square, 6:59 p.m.

Washington Square, 7:01 p.m.

Washington Square, 7:03 p.m.

Washington Square, 7:12 p.m.

Since 1981, I have watched, followed, interviewed, and photographed street performers. I began by simply documenting the performers' shows, but I was soon impressed by the variety of ingenious strategies these performers had devised to do theatre *outside*—both literally and metaphorically. Forgoing the sanctity of a walled theater space, with darkened auditorium, fixed seating, prepaid audiences, and reassuring reviews, the street performer instead engages and manipulates the urban environment, using its traffic, noise, and passersby as props for his shows. Buses rumble by; helicopters hover overhead; hecklers interrupt the rhythm of the performance; rain, cold, or police can defeat the performer entirely. The audience surrounds the street performer, restless, waiting, impatient. Yet the street performer succeeds in transforming urban *space* into a theater *place*, turning visitors resting on steps into an audience seated on bleachers.

An outdoor performer's skills rely on his ability to incorporate the urban environment and make it part of the show. Vera "hides" in the crowd when sirens wail in the distance. Street mime Peter Shub uses a taxi and its passengers to amuse a ready-made audience on the Metropolitan Museum of Art's steps. Each performer cultivates his environment—allowing its actions to impinge upon his actions—and then develops ways to control or order the seeming chaos around him. Explains street magician Bert Lee: "You have to create all things possible out of that which is available. . . . You develop a feeling for people, but there is always the X factor, like a line of fire trucks going by" (in Heise, 1983: 83). The street performer's text nevertheless appears natural, flexible, and spontaneous. His show corresponds to present modes of feeling and is accessible to all who wander through the open space of his performances. Unlike the street musician, who simply places a spare change receptacle on the sidewalk and plays music, the street performer learns to decrease the critical aesthetic distance most familiar to and comfortable for an indoor, passive audience.

In the final analysis, the street performer relies on the most fundamental contract of the theater—the central yet unspoken agreement between the solo performer and the individual spectator: "I will watch," the spectator's presence implies, "as long as you are worth watching." "I will be worth watching," the performer's actions respond, "as long as you watch."[3] Together, spectator and performer define the relationship that is performance. Outdoors especially, it is the spectator who allows performance to occur. No spectators = No performance.

Thus, though civic authorities argue about sidewalk congestion, the street performer simply learns to work within the fundamental theatrical pattern of gathering, performing, and dispersing. As city planners ponder the appropriateness of certain locations for outdoor performance or deliberate the necessity for scheduling shows, street performers construct a self-regulating activity. As mayors contemplate potential licensing strategies, street performers receive permission to perform from the laughter and contributions of their audiences.

Street performance restores theater's ability to communicate with pure forces. The street performer's show, happening here and now,

3. The phrasing for this contract was first presented by Hollis Huston, a former street performer, in a guest lecture at the University of Texas at Dallas. Huston added, however, that his idea for the fundamental performance contract was inspired by one of my articles on street performance (Harrison, 1984).

using us and our environment as props for its action, both entertains and enchants us largely because it takes place so directly within our shared environment. In fact, the transformations that occur in street performance may be more "real" than indoor ones. The transcendent power of the outdoor entertainer's show is achieved using the real people, objects, smells, feelings, sounds, and restrictions of the built environment. The heat from Tony Vera's fire is *really* hot—audiences lean back in fright as the flames near their faces; the noise from an approaching siren is not a taped sound effect; the nearby vendor has not been sent by Central Casting—the smell of his hot dogs and sauerkraut is real, authentic, present. Perhaps, then, as Antonin Artaud once declared, "it is not upon the stage that the true is to be sought nowadays, but in the street" (1958: 76).

Milo Max, Washington Square Park

References

Alexander, Ron
    1983   "Sidewalks Paved with Talent." *New York Times*, November 4: C1, 24.

Altman, Irwin, and Chemers, Martin
    1980   *Culture and Environment*. Monterey, Calif.: Brooks/Cole Publishing Company.

Anderson, David
    1961   "Folk Singers Get Another Chance." *New York Times*, May 13: 1, 11.

Artaud, Antonin
    1958   *The Theatre and Its Double*. New York: Grove Press.

Bachelard, Gaston
    1964   *The Poetics of Space*. New York: Orion Press.

Baird, Stephen, ed.
    1983   *Street Performer's Newsletter*, June.

Battiata, Mary
    1981   "Musicians Given Access to Alexandria Sidewalks." *Washington Post*, August 14: B1, 5.

Bauman, Richard
    1977   *Verbal Art as Performance*. Cambridge, Mass.: Newbury House Publishers.

Benamou, Michel, and Caramello, Charles
    1977   *Performance in Postmodern Culture*. Madison, Wisc.: Coda Press.

Benedikt, Michael, and Wellwarth, George, eds.
    1966   *Modern French Theatre*. New York: E. P. Dutton and Co.

Benjamin, Philip
    1964   "Washington Square Gets a New Plan." *New York Times*, October 28: 47.

Blumer, Herbert
    1946   "Collective Behavior." In A. M. Lee, ed., *New Outline of the*

Principles of Sociology. New York: Barnes and Noble, pp. 165–220.

Bouissac, Paul
   1976   *Circus and Culture: A Semiotic Approach.* Bloomington: Indiana University Press.

Boyle, Wickham
   1978   *On the Streets: A Guide to New York City's Buskers.* New York: New York City Department of Cultural Affairs.

Brantley, Robin
   1978   "All the World's Their Stage on Fifth Avenue and the Mall." *New York Times,* June 9: C21.

Brook, Peter
   1968   *The Empty Space.* New York: Avon Books.

Burke, Kenneth
   1969   *A Grammar of Motives.* Berkeley: University of California Press.

Campbell, Patricia J.
   1981   *Passing the Hat: Street Performers in America.* New York: Delacorte Press.

Cantor, Mindy, ed.
   1982   *Around the Square, 1830–1890.* New York: New York University Press.

Chadwick, Bruce
   1982   "One Big Lincoln Center." *Daily News,* April 27: 1, 3.

Chambers, E. K.
   1903   *The Mediaeval Stage,* Vols. 1 and 2. Oxford: Clarendon Press.

Chapin, Anna Alice
   1920   *Greenwich Village.* New York: Dodd, Mead and Company.

Claflin, Edward, and Sheridan, Jeff
   1977   *Street Magic: An Illustrated History of Wandering Magicians and Their Conjuring Arts.* New York: Dolphin Books.

Clark, Sidney Wrangel
   1929   *The Annals of Conjuring.* London: George Johnson.

Cohen, David, and Greenwood, Ben
   1981   *The Buskers: A History of Street Entertainment.* North Pomfret, Vt.: David and Charles.

Cohen, Joe
   1983   "Street Performers Emboldened by Success of Fellow Busker." *Variety,* September 28: 161.

Collins, Sherwood
   1973   "Boston's Political Street Theatre: The 18th Century Pope Day

Pageants." *Educational Theatre Journal*, December: 401–3.
Condos, Susan
    1976   "Jeff Sheridan's Street Magic," *Drama Review* (T-70), Vol. 20, No. 2, June: 56–58.
Conley, Robert
    1961   "Folk Singing Arrest Stirs 2,000." *New York Times*, May 1: 1.
Csikszentimihalyi, Mihaly
    1977   *Beyond Boredom and Anxiety*. San Francisco: Jossey-Bass Publishers.
Dublin Evening Press
    1975   "A Human Jukebox Who Just Doesn't Slot In." August 20: 5.
Feldman, Jay
    1983   "Sunday Afternoon at Washington Square: A Nostalgic Event." *Bluegrass Unlimited*, Vol. 17, No. 9, March: 21–25.
Fincher, Jack
    1972   "Mime in the Streets." *Saturday Review*, August 12: 39–41.
Geist, William E.
    1984   "Street Theatre: From Buskers to Fire Eaters." *New York Times*, July 11: B3.
Goddard, J. R.
    1961   "'Right to Sing Rally' Scores Ban by Morris: Ready to Fight." *Village Voice*, Vol. 6, No. 26, April 20: 1, 13.
Gralla, Preston
    1978   "All the Street's a Stage." *Boston Globe*, New England Magazine, August 13: 3–15, 29.
Greenhouse, Stephen
    1984   "Chicago Trying to Restrict Street Performers." *New York Times*, September 10: A19.
Hall, Edward T.
    1969   *The Hidden Dimension*. New York: Doubleday Publishers.
Harrison, Sally
    1984   "Drawing a Circle in Washington Square." *Studies in Visual Communication*, Vol. 10, No. 2, Spring: 68–83.
Harrison-Pepper, Sally
    1987   "Folk Heroes of the Urban Environment: Street Performers in the American City." *Urban Resources*, Vol. 4, No. 3, Spring: 7–12.
Heckscher, August
    1977   *Open Spaces: The Life of American Cities*. New York: Harper & Row, Publishers.

Heise, Karen
   1983 "Street Performers Weather City's Regulations." *Chicago Tribune*, August 5: B3.

Hoelterhoff, Manuela
   1977 "All the World Is Indeed a Stage." *Wall Street Journal*, September 9: 10.

Hofmann, Paul
   1961 "Singers Return to Park in Peace." *New York Times*, May 15: 27.

Huxtable, Ada Louise
   1943 "Just a Little Love, a Little Care." *New York Times*, December 9: 2.
   1964 "Test Case in Park Planning." *New York Times*, October 28: 48.

James, Michael
   1959 "Free Show in Washington Square Is a Hit." *New York Times*, May 25: 1, 34.

James, William
   1890 *The Principles of Psychology*. New York: Holt.

Jason, Ray
   1978–79 "The Joys of Street Performing." *Co-Evolution Quarterly*, No. 20, Winter: 56–60.

Jusserand, J. J.
   1950 *English Wayfaring Life in the Middle Ages*, 4th Edition. New York: George Putnam's Sons.

Kirshenblatt-Gimblett, Barbara
   1983 "The Future of Folklore Studies in America: The Urban Frontier." *Folklore Forum*, Vol. 16, No. 2: 175–234.

Kornfeld, Barry
   1959 "Folk Singing in Washington Square." *Caravan*, No. 18, August–September: 6–11.

Kriegsman, Alan M.
   1984 "This Thing Called Mime." *Washington Post*, July 8: H1.

Langer, Suzanne K.
   1953 *Feeling and Form*. New York: Charles Scribner's Sons.

Leach, Edmund
   1976 *Culture and Communication: The Logic by Which Symbols Are Connected*. Cambridge: Cambridge University Press.

Lichtenstein, Grace
   1974 "Stuntman, Eluding Guards, Walks a Tightrope between Trade Center Towers." *New York Times*, August 8: 20.

Lipman, Joanne
  1983 "Street Musicians Get Sizable Rewards." *Wall Street Journal*, October 7: 1, 22.

McCabe, James
  1971 *Lights and Shadows of New York Life*. London: Andre Deutsch.

McGuigan, Cathleen, et al.
  1984 "The Sidewalk Vaudevillians." *Newsweek*, September 24: 83.

McKechnie, Samuel
  1931 *Popular Entertainment through the Ages*. New York: Frederick A. Stokes Company.

McNamara, Brooks
  1975 "The Busker." *Greater London Arts*, No. 85, September–October: 9–10.
  1976 *Step Right Up*. New York: Doubleday and Company.

McNamara, Brooks; Rojo, Jerry; and Schechner, Richard
  1975 *Theatres, Spaces, and Environments: Eighteen Projects*. New York: Drama Books Specialists.

Milgram, Stanley, and Toch, Hans
  1969 "Collective Behavior: Crowds and Social Movements." In Lindzey Gardner and Elliot Aronson, eds., *Handbook of Social Psychology*, Vol. 1. Reading, Mass.: Addison-Wesley Publishing Company.

Millstein, Gilbert
  1958 "New Battle of Our Village Square." *New York Times Magazine*, May 4: 32–38.

Mukarovsky, Jan
  1977 *Structure, Sign, and Function*, ed. and trans. John Burbank and Peter Steiner. New Haven: Yale University Press.

New York Times
  1935 "Hurdy Gurdy Fees Abolished by Mayor." March 8: 23.
  1961 "City Acts to Silence Minstrels' Playing in Washington Square." March 28: 37.
  1961a "Folk Singers Riot in Washington Sq." April 10: 1.
  1961b "'Villagers' Score Park Folk Singing." May 19: 25.
  1961c "Folk Singing Ban Upset on Appeal." July 7: 11.
  1977 "Street Theater's Appeal as Big as All Outdoors." April 20: B1.
  1983 "Chicago Considers Permitting Artists' Performances in Streets." April 15: 2.

New Yorker
  1975 "Five New York Street Musicians." September 29: 39–40.

1979 "Discovering the Steinettes." July 2: 78–81.
1980 "Steve and Carol." August 11: 24–25.
1982 "Street Music." August 23: 23–24.
1983 "Winging It." March 28: 41–43.

Nichols, Mary Perot
1961 "Morris Ban on Singers in Square Divides Village." *Village Voice*, April 27: 1, 16.

Nichols, Robert
1962 "Making Our Parks Safe for Howitzers." *Village Voice*, March 29: 1, 15.
1962a "Troglodytes on the Grass, Alas." *Village Voice*, April 5: 2, 6.

Pavis, Patrice
1982 *Languages of the Stage*. New York: Performing Arts Journal Publications.

People magazine
1983 "Rubber-faced and Razor-tongued, Street Comedian Charlie Barnett Steps Up to the Silver Screen." November 24: 94.

Petit, Philippe
1979 "The Vagabond Theatre." *Village Voice*, July 2: 58.

Petit, Philippe, and Reddy, John
1975 "Two Towers, I Walk." *Reader's Digest*, April: 204–27.

Preziosi, Donald
1979 *The Semiotics of the Built Environment*. Bloomington: Indiana University Press.

Rapoport, Amos
1977 *Human Aspects of Urban Form: Towards a Man-Environment Approach to Urban Form and Design*. Oxford: Pergamon Press.

Richardson, Clem
1984 "Rush Street Wants a Break." *Chicago Sun Times*, June 11: 8.

Robertson, Nan
1961 "Court Backs Folk-Singing Ban by City in Washington Square." *New York Times*, May 5: 1, 19.
1961a "600 Sing in Square but without Guitars." *New York Times*, May 8: 1, 41.

Schechner, Richard
1969 *Public Domain*. Indianapolis: Bobbs-Merrill Company.
1973 *Environmental Theatre*. New York: Hawthorn Books.
1977 *Essays on Performance Theory, 1970–1976*. New York: Drama Book Specialists.

1981 "Performers and Spectators Transported and Transformed." *Kenyon Review*, Vol. 3, No. 4, Fall: 83–113.
1982 *The End of Humanism*. New York: Performing Arts Journal Publications.

Sibley, John
1964 "Village Angered by Rising Number of Derelicts in Washington Square." *New York Times*, September 21: 33.

Simon, Peter Angelo
1978 *Big Apple Circus*. New York: Penguin Books.

Smith, Howard
1981 "Wild in the Streets." *Village Voice*, September 10: 15.

Smith, Zay
1982 "Keeping Music off the Streets." *Chicago Sun Times*, July 18: 62–63.

Southern, Richard
1961 *The Seven Ages of the Theatre*. New York: Hill and Wang.

Stengren, Bernard
1963 "Design Is Ordered in Washington Square." *New York Times*, June 13: 35.

Sypher, Wylie
1956 *Comedy*. New York: Doubleday and Company.

Talese, Gay
1964 "Washington Square Park: Melting Pot of the Village." *New York Times*, June 8: 31.

Taylor, Lisa, ed.
1979 *Urban Open Spaces*. New York: Cooper Hewitt Museum.

Time magazine
1979 "The Bands of Summer." August 27: 66.

Turner, Victor
1982 *From Ritual to Theatre*. New York: Performing Arts Journal Publications.

Variety
1983 "N.Y. Street Scene: Agencies Now Cover Performing Urchins." August 3: 1, 66.
1983a "Charlie Barnett." August 17: 84.

Village Voice
1961 "Keep It Safe for Buses!" April 13: 4.

Wallace, Samuel E.
1980 *The Urban Environment*. Chicago: Dorsey Press.

Whyte, William H.
- 1974 "The Best Street Life in the World." *New York* magazine, July 15: 27–33.
- 1980 *The Social Life of Small Urban Spaces.* Washington, D.C.: Conservation Foundation.
- 1988 *City: Rediscovering the Center.* New York: Doubleday.

Wilson, Susan
- 1984 "Street Performing Isn't 'Easy Street' to Fame and Fortune." *Boston Globe,* Calendar Section, June 21: 12.

Wolfe, Gerard R.
- 1975 *New York: A Guide to the Metropolis.* New York: New York University Press.

Zigun, Dick D.
- 1983 "The Street Dancer, or, How to Make Money by Making a Scene." *Daily News,* June 15.

Zorn, Eric
- 1984 "Newly Licensed Performers Cash in on the Street." *Chicago Tribune,* June 1: E1.

Zucker, Paul
- 1959 *Town and Square: From the Agora to the Village Green.* New York: Columbia University Press.

Correspondence and Interviews

The following individuals or groups worked as street performers between 1980 and 1984. Their performance specializations and primary geographic area(s) are indicated in parentheses. Interview dates precede each listing.

June 22, 1984	Rick Aralias (comedian, Washington Square Park)
October 23, 1981	Carl Asche (storyteller, various)
July 24, 1984	Stephen Baird (musician, Boston/Cambridge, and editor of the *Street Performer's Newsletter*).
1981–84	Charlie Barnett (comedian, Washington Square Park)
June 1, 1984	Blair (magician, Washington Square Park)
September 1982	Vincent Brady (steel piano, New York City)
June 1983	The Brewery Puppets (puppets, Washington Square Park)
April 27, 1983	Mitchell Cohen (turtle racing, New York City)
August 7, 1982	Steve Fogelman (acrobat, Washington Square Park)
May 27, 1984	Jim Gardner (escapologist, Washington Square Park)
September 5, 1983	Flip Golson (acrobat, New Haven, Connecticut)
May 27, 1984	Mike Inserra (juggler, Washington Square Park)
June 2, 1984	Timothy Ivory (ropewalker, Sixth Avenue, New York City)

Correspondence and Interviews

July 18, 1982	Don Littlejohn (mime/magician, New York Public Library)
May–June 1984	Cotton MacAloon (juggler, Washington Square Park)
May 26, 1984	Milo Max (clown, Washington Square Park)
1981–84	Steve and Carol Mills (unicyclists/jugglers, Father Demo Square, Sheridan Square, and Washington Square Park)
July 28, 1984	Albert Owens (comedian, Washington Square Park)
August 1982	Philippe Petit (ropewalker, Washington Square Park)
1981–84	Nguyen Bien Phuc Chang (juggler, Washington Square Park and Philadelphia, Pennsylvania)
November 1983	Kirk Reeves (musician, Boston)
August 12, 1984	Jeff Sheridan (street magician, Central Park, and co-author with Edward Claflin, *Street Magic*)
June–July 1984	Peter Shub (mime, Paris, Philadelphia and New York)
April 1983	Slap Happy (puppets/music, Boston and New York)
November 1983	Will Soto (juggler, Chicago)
April 14, 1983	The Steinettes (singers, Sheridan Square, New York)
May 27, 1984	Thriller (dancers, Washington Square Park)
1981–85	Tony Vera (fireblower, Washington Square Park)
May 1981	Timothy Williams (mime, Washington Square Park)

ADDITIONAL INTERVIEWS AND/OR CORRESPONDENCE

September 1984	Patricia Campbell, author of *Passing the Hat*
August 10, 1984	Richard Campbell, fan of Charlie Barnett
July–September 1984	Alan Cohen, attorney (Alexandria, Virginia)
August 8, 1984	Howard Smith, columnist for the *Village Voice*
	New York City audiences
	New York City police

Index

Acrobats, xv, 15, 41, 72–73, 75, 82–86
Alexander, Ron, 12, 44
Alexandria, Virginia, xii, 34–35
Altman, Irwin, 57–58
American Civil Liberties Union, 32–34
Amusement parks, 66
Anderson, David, 26
Anderson, Harry, 17
Apollinaire, Guillaume, 68
Artaud, Antonin, 68, 142
Asche, Carl, xiii, 11, 114, 115
Aspen, Judge Marvin E., 33
Audience: participation, xiv, 4, 29, 37, 78, 88–90, 95–96, 106–9, 111–12; views of street performance, 4–5, 9, 11, 16, 19, 27, 72, 74, 96, 113

Bachelard, Gaston, 131
Baird, Stephen, ix, 12, 17, 18, 26, 36–38
Barnett, Charlie, 17, 19, 78, 84, 116, 118, 120; and hecklers, 95, 96, 99, 115; notoriety of, 77, 92, 99–100; performances: analysis of (based on aerial photographs), 126, 128–29, 136; documentation of, 92–100; location for, 58, 75, 93–94, 126, 128
Battiata, Mary, 34
Bauman, Richard, 19, 96, 117
Begging, 22–23, 25, 26, 31, 92. *See also* Laws; Licenses; Police
Benamou, Michel, 20, 71

Benedikt, Michael, 68
Benjamin, Philip, 52
Blair, 73, 75
Blumer, Herbert, 124
Bonnien, Paul, 78
Boston/Cambridge, Massachusetts, 11, 12, 15, 17–18; overview of street performance in, 36–38
Bouissac, Paul, ix, 119–22
Boyle, Wickham, 12, 14, 21
Brady, Victor, 43
Brantley, Robin, 41
Breakdancers and breakdancing, 6, 32–33, 73, 76–77, 128–29
Brewery Puppet Troupe, 44, 73–75
Brook, Peter, 131
Brother Blue (Hugh Hill), 15
Bruno, Richard, 21
Bryan, Judge Albert V., Jr., 30, 34–35
Bunraku, 75
Burke, Kenneth, 126
Butterfly Man (Robert Armstrong), 28
Byrne, Jane M., 31

Campbell, Patricia, ix, 11, 15, 28–30, 36, 37, 78
Cantor, Mindy, 49
Caramello, Charles, 20, 71
Carson, Johnny, 17
Chadwick, Bruce, 44
Chambers, E. K., 22
Chang, xi, 16, 84, 114, 118, 120; performances: analysis of (based on

156 INDEX

Chang (*continued*)
  aerial photographs), 128–36; documentation of, 78–82; location for, xi, 58, 75, 78–80, 126, 128
Chapin, Anna, 51
Chemers, Martin, 57–58
Chicago, Illinois, xii, 15; overview of street performance in, 31–34
Circus, 17, 42, 82, 112, 116, 119–22
Claflin, Edward, 12, 22
Clark, Sidney, 22, 23
Cohen, Alan, 34–35
Cohen, David, xii, 21, 22
Cohen, Joe, 100
Cohen, Mitchell, x, xi, 7, 78, 94, 114, 115, 116, 119; on bravery, 19, 92; motives for performing, xiii, 12–14, 85–86, 92; performances: documentation of, 86–92; location for, xi, 58, 74, 86, 92, 126
Collins, Sherwood, 23
Commedia Dell'Arte, 115
Condos, Susan, 118
Conley, Robert, 25
Crowd control, 34–35, 125–26
Csikszentmihalyi, Mihaly, 13–14

Daley, Richard J., Sr., 31
Davenport, Lee, 30, 34–35
Decroux, Etienne, 5–6

Environmental theatre, 27, 114–15, 124–25

Feldman, Jay, 24
Fincher, Jack, 14
Flow (and performance), 13–14
Fogelman, Steve, 3, 15, 72–73
Folk Singers' "Riot," 24–26
Friedrich, William, 33

Gardner, Jim, 14, 73, 77
Geist, William, 41

Goddard, J. R., 25
Golson, Flip, 73, 75
Gralla, Preston, 15
Greenhouse, Stephen, 33
Greenwood, Ben, xii, 21, 22
Grossman, Harvey, 33–34
Gruenberg, Ron, 17

Hall, Edward T., ix, 63
Hecht, Justice William C., Jr., 25–26
Heckscher, August, 46–47
Heise, Karen, 9, 141
Hoelterhoff, Manuela, 43
Hofmann, Paul, 25
Hokum, Jeebs, 28
Human Jukebox (Grimes Poznikov), 28–29
Hurdy Gurdy players, 23–24
Huston, Hollis, 141 n
Huxtable, Ada Louise, 51, 53

Income. *See* Pitch; Street Performers, potential earnings of
Inserra, Mike, 73, 75

Jackson, Michael, 76
James, Michael, 24
James, William, 18
Jason, Ray, 10, 28
Jauss, H. R., 114
Jugglers and juggling, xi, xii, xiv, xv, 120–22, 125; Boston, 37; Chicago, 31–32; history of, 22–23; New York City, 39, 43, 75; San Francisco, 28, Washington Square, 78–85, 120–22. *See also* specific acts
Jusserand, J. J., 22

Kaplow, Bruce, 16
Kirshenblatt-Gimblett, Barbara, ix, xiii, 55
Koch, Edward, 25, 44
Kornfeld, Barry, 24

Index

La Guardia, Fiorello, 24, 38
Labowitz, Kenneth, 34–35
Langer, Suzanne K., 122
Laws, xiii, 22–39, 42, 44. *See also* Begging; Licenses; Police
Leach, Edmund, 97
Levey, Paul, 30, 32
Licenses, 23, 27; pros and cons of, 36–38; in Washington Square, 24–26, 59. *See also* Begging; Laws; Police
Lichtenstein, Grace, 42
Liminal space, 70–71, 71n
Lipman, Joanne, 44
Littlejohn, Don, 5, 11, 39, 72
Lynch, Kevin, 12

MacAloon, Cotton, 5, 73, 75–76
McCabe, James, 23
McKechnie, Samuel, 15
McNamara, Brooks, ix, 16, 23, 114, 118
Magic and magicians, xi, xii, xiv, 118, 141; Boston, 39; Chicago, 31–32; history of, 21–24; New York City, 43, 44; San Francisco, 29; Washington Square, 75, 120–22. *See also* specific acts
Magic circle, xi, 121–22, 126–27
Marceau, Marcel, 6, 74
Max, Milo, 15, 73, 74, 143
Medicine Show, 16, 118
Mikotowicz, Tom, ix, 73, 127, 129–30
Milgram, Stanley, 127
Mills, Steve and Carol, xi, 16, 43, 78, 94, 116, 118; performances: documentation of, 82–86; location for, xi, 58–60, 75, 82–83, 126
Millstein, Gilbert, 49–50, 53–54
Mime, 4–6, 14, 31–32, 39, 41, 43, 72–74, 103–15, 128–29, 132
Moody, Reverend Howard, 25–26
Morris, Newbold, 24–26, 51–52

Mosier, Joe, ix, 127
Moses, Robert, 51
Mountebanks, 23
Mozart on Fifth, 41

Ned and Will, 85
New York City (Manhattan), xi, xii, 8–12, 16, 19, 26–28, 64, 71, 77, 94, 97, 122; overview of street performance in, 38–44; street performance areas: Battery Park, 92; Bleecker Street, 6–7, 98; Bryant Park, 9, 98; Central Park, 39–42, 44, 75, 77; Chinatown, 39–40; Citicorp Center, 9; Columbus Avenue, 38; Coney Island, 7; Father Demo Square, 6; Fifth Avenue, xii, 6, 9, 39–41, 46, 48–49, 51, 53, 92, 130; Greenwich Village, 7, 17, 39–40, 50–52, 82, 85; Metropolitan Museum of Art, 4, 6, 9, 17, 39–41, 43–44, 86, 140–41; Museum of Natural History, 39–41; Public Library, 8, 11, 39–41, 44, 72, 86; Rockefeller Center, 44; St. Patrick's Cathedral, 8; Sheridan Square, 6–7, 43, 82, 84, 98; Sixth Avenue, 19, 79, 86; South Street Seaport, 7; Times Square, 39–40, 43–44, 74; Wall Street, 39–40, 86; World Trade Center, 42, 44, 96
New York University, ix, xv, 46, 48, 56, 59, 127
Nichols, Mary Perot, 51
Nichols, Robert, 52

Oleszko, Pat, 12
Olmsted, Frederick Law, 48, 64
Owens, Albert, 73, 77

Pavis, Patrice, 114
Performance ring, 58, 63, 66–68, 72, 76–77, 78, 83, 127–40

Performance strategies: developing an act, 72–74, 78–81, 98–99, 117; drag outs, 112, 116; flexibility, 114; location choice, 9–10, 74–77; preparatory routines, 3–5, 7, 19, 39, 80; street performance "text," 115–17, 120–21, 123, 141–42. *See also* Pitch; Street Performance; specific acts

Petit Philippe, 17–19, 37–38, 42–43, 59, 73, 74, 98, 116, 126

Phuc, Nguyen Bien. *See* Chang

Pitch (money gathering strategy), 5, 7, 8, 39, 41, 77, 81, 85, 90–92, 97–98, 113, 116, 121. *See also* Begging; Laws; Licenses; Street Performers, potential earnings of

Police (confrontations with), 6–9, 24–26, 29–30, 32, 36–39, 42–44, 77, 102. *See also* Begging; Laws; Licenses

Poznikov, Grimes, 28–29

Preziosi, Donald, 71

Punch and Judy shows, 23

Rapoport, Amos, 66

Richardson, Clem, 32

Robertson, Nan, 25–26

Rojo, Jerry, 114

Rosie Radiator and the Pushrods, 28

Rothenberg, Jerome, 20

San Francisco, California, xi, 10, 14, 17, 26, 27; overview of street performance in, 28–30

Schechner, Richard, ix, xvi, 27, 68, 114, 115, 124–25

Shakespeare Brothers, 11, 37, 38

Sheridan, Jeff, 12, 22, 118

Shields, Robert, 14, 17

Sibley, John, 52

Shub, Peter, xi, xiii, 15, 19–20, 116, 122, 140–41; performance documentation, 3–10

Slap Happy, 18

Smith, David, 31

Smith, Howard, 95, 98–99

Smith, Zay, 31

Sociofugal and sociopetal space, 63, 64, 68

Soto, Will, 9

Southern, Richard, xii, 45

Steinettes, 15, 17, 43

Stengren, Bernard, 52

Street Musicians, xi, 17, 141; basic performance structure of, xiv; Boston, 36; Chicago, 31; compared to street performers, xiv; historical overview of, 22–26; New York City, 9, 39, 41, 43–44; motives of, xiv

Street Performance: effect of urban space upon, xiii, xv, 45, 114–15, 140–42; and "being discovered," 17–18, 99–100; benefits to cities, xi–xii, 23–24, 32, 35, 38, 43–44, 71, 122–23; civic perception of, xii, 9, 21, 24, 27, 141 (*See also* specific cities); compared to indoor theatre, xiii–xvi, 7, 9, 10, 16–20, 77, 83, 99, 114–19, 125–26, 140–42; compared to street music, xiv; fundamental contract of, 141; history of, xii, 21–26; immediacy of, 9, 12, 14; and merchants, xii, 29–35, 38; sideshows, 72–77; territoriality of, 26–27, 37, 38–42, 58–59, 73–78, 80, 83, 86, 102; "text," 115–17, 120–21, 123, 141; U.S. locations for, 15, 17, 26–27, 35, 75 (*See also* specific cities). *See also* Audiences; Begging; Crowd Control; Flow; Laws; Licenses; Performance Strategies; Pitch; Police; Street Performers

Street Performers: and freedom, 10–12, 30, 114; and gender, xi; and heroism, xv, 19–20, 37–38, 92, 119–21; hopes and fears of, 9–13; motives of, xiii, 9–13, 17–19, 72; potential earnings of, 7–9, 11, 16–17, 24, 31, 86, 90–92, 98, 113, 116 (*See also* Pitch). *See also* Acrobats; Jugglers and juggling; Flow; Magic and magicians; Mime; Performance Strategies; Street Performance; specific acts and cities
Swami, 76

Talese, Gay, 54–55
Taylor, Lisa, 13
Theatre for the New City, 129–30
Thriller (dance group), 73, 76
Toch, Hans, 127
Turner, Victor, 64, 71
Turtle racing. *See* Mitchell Cohen
Tweed, William Marcy, 48, 51

Vera, Tony, ix, xi, xv, 3, 16, 100, 116–17, 140, 142; effect on other performers, 7, 59, 75–76, 78, 80, 84, 94, 98, 114, 126–36; authority in the square, 5, 7, 58–59, 74–76, 81, 83, 86; folk hero, xv, 120–21; "king" of Washington Square, xv, 18, 42, 59, 101; performances: analysis of (based on aerial photographs), 126–36; documentation of, 101–23; location for, xi, 58, 63, 80, 101–3, 126, 128

Wagner, Robert (Chicago Police Lieutenant), 32
Wagner, Robert (New York City Mayor), 26, 52
Wallace, Samuel, 46
Washington Square Park: aerial photographs of, 132–40; compared to Central Park, 41–42; concentric rings of activity in, 68–69, 71; design elements in, 46–53, 63–68; folk singer's "riot" in, 24–26; historical overview of, 45–55; movement patterns in, 54, 59–71, 131–40; performance ring, 58, 64, 66–69, 72, 76–77, 78, 83, 127–40; "square" versus "park," 46–47; territories in, 56–59, 68–71. *See also* New York City; specific acts
Wellwarth, George, 68
White, Stanford, 49
Whyte, William H., xii, 9, 33, 35, 41, 43–44, 101
William Morris Agency, 17, 99
Williams, Robin, 17, 99
Williams, Timothy, 73–74
Wynbrandt, Robert, 31

Young, Israel, 26

Zobel, Judge Rya, 30
Zucker, Paul, 47